WISCONSIN

STATE PARKS BUCKET LIST

Max Kukis Galgan

ISBN: 9798758791165
Copyright © X 2023

Thank you for buying my book!
I hope you like it.

Your feedback is important to me, and I would greatly appreciate it if you could take a moment to share your thoughts by leaving an online review.

Your review will not only help me improve as an author but also assist other potential readers in making informed decisions.

Once again, thank you for your support and for considering leaving a review.

Warm regards,
Max

ABOUT WISCONSIN

Wisconsin became an American territory after the American Revolution and soon thereafter began attracting settlers seeking work in its mining, timber, and dairy industries. It was admitted to the union as the 30th state in 1848. In the years leading up to the Civil War, Wisconsin was an important stop on the Underground Railroad, with many slaves passing through the state on their way to freedom in Canada.

Today, Wisconsin is a leader in dairy production and is known for its high-quality cheddar cheese - residents sometimes refer to themselves as "cheeseheads." Famous Wisconsin residents include architect Frank Lloyd Wright, magician Harry Houdini, and U.S. Army General Douglas MacArthur.

More than 12,000 years ago, the area of present-day Wisconsin was covered by huge glaciers. During Wisconsin's glacial stage, when the ice sheet began to melt, it left behind scenic physical features, including sand plains, terminal and basin moraines, drumlins, oases, and low-lying areas that became lakes. In October 1871, the most destructive forest fire in American history broke out in Wisconsin: 1,200 people died and 2 billion trees burned in the fire known as the Great Peshtigo Fire. Wisconsin's climate is characterized by long, cold winters and warm, relatively short summers. Forests once covered more than four-fifths of the state, with the remainder being prairies and wetlands. Most of the forests have been cleared for timber and agricultural crops, but as a result of natural regrowth and reforestation, about two-fifths of Wisconsin is reforested.

About nine-tenths of Wisconsin's population comes from northern Europe. Those of German descent are the most numerous, followed by those of Irish, Polish, Scandinavian (mainly Norwegian), and British descent. African-Americans are the largest minority group in Wisconsin, making up about 6% of the population. Native Americans make up less than 1 percent of the population. There are towns with fewer than 1,000 residents throughout the state, but about two-thirds of Wisconsinites live in urban areas. Most people live in the Southeast, where eastern migrants first arrived and settled.

The three major economic enterprises of the state of Wisconsin are manufacturing, agriculture and tourism. Agriculture in Wisconsin is primarily based on intensive dairy production. Manufacturing is mainly engaged in the processing of agricultural products, as well as the production of metal products and forest products. Milwaukee and the surrounding area is one of the major manufacturing centers in the state, which in addition to brewing specializes in the production of electrical machinery and equipment. Tourism emerged as a major industry in the 1950s.

Wisconsin is a place where you can explore pristine lakes, miles of scenic hiking trails, and stunning natural wonders. About 120,000 acres (50,000 hectares) of state parks and millions of acres of national, state, and county forests are available for recreational use in the state of Wisconsin. Most of the public forests are in the north, although there is a park within an hour's drive of almost every place in the state. The sparsely populated, heavily forested northern Glacier region is the epitome of the Northwoods, with clear streams and hundreds of lakes for fishing and water sports. Whether you enjoy outdoor activities like hiking, biking, fishing, canoeing, or indoor activities like shopping, museums, and art galleries, you won't be disappointed.

Among the more interesting vacation areas is the Door Peninsula, between Lake Michigan and Green Bay, with miles of rocky coastline and sandy beaches and five state parks. It is largely forested, with summer cottages, small seaside villages, craft stores, and summer theater. One of the least known areas of the state, but deserving of more attention, is the scenic mountainous and valley country of the Western Highlands, with steep wooded slopes, bare rock cliffs and towers, tree-lined side roads winding through quiet pastoral scenes that include many Amish farms and the preserved homes of Cornish lead miners at Mineral Point and at Merrimac, the only surviving car ferry across the Wisconsin River.

A vacation in Wisconsin can put you close to the Kettle Moraine State Forest, which has excellent biking trails. Or choose Wisconsin's Apostle Islands - kayakers will love exploring Lake Superior's many caves and shipwrecks.

Food lovers will love to try as many Wisconsin artisan cheeses as possible. You can drive from cheesemaker to cheesemaker or choose to vacation in Wisconsin in a city with a good farmers market - then the cheesemakers will bring their wares to you. And what pairs better with craft cheeses than craft beer? In Milwaukee, take a tour and tasting at Lakefront and Sprecher breweries.

Wisconsin Dells is a classic family vacation destination. Wisconsin Dells vacations will put you close to all the action - you'll have to pry the kids away from the amusement parks, wave pools, and water parks in Wisconsin Dells!

Lake Geneva boasts clean beaches, golf, and a small-town atmosphere that is sure to appeal to city dwellers - it's a popular destination for Chicago residents.

PARK NAME	COUNTY	EST.	VISITED
Amnicon Falls State Park	Douglas	1961	
Aztalan State Park	Jefferson	1947	
Belmont Mound State Park	Lafayette	1961	
Big Bay State Park	Ashland	1963	
Big Foot Beach State Park	Walworth	1949	
Black River State Forest	Jackson	1957	
Blue Mound State Park	Dane	1959	
Brule River State Forest	Douglas	1907	
Brunet Island State Park	Chippewa	1936	
Buckhorn State Park	Juneau	1971	
Cadiz Springs State Recreation Area	Green	1970	
Capital Springs State Recreation Area	Dane	2000	
Chippewa Flowage	Sawyer	1923	
Chippewa Moraine State Recreation Area	Chippewa	1971	
Copper Culture State Park	Oconto	1959	
Copper Falls State Park	Ashland	1929	
Coulee Experimental State Forest	La Crosse	1960	
Council Grounds State Park	Lincoln	1938	
Cross Plains State Park	Dane	1971	
Devil's Lake State Park	Sauk	1911	
Fischer Creek State Recreation Area	Manitowoc	1991	
Flambeau River State Forest	Sawyer, Price	1930	
Governor Dodge State Park	Iowa	1948	
Governor Earl Peshtigo River State Forest	Marinette	2001	
Governor Knowles State Forest	Burnett, Polk	1970	
Governor Nelson State Park	Dane	1975	
Governor Thompson State Park	Marinette	2000	
Harrington Beach State Park	Ozaukee	1966	

PARK NAME	COUNTY	EST.	VISITED
Hartman Creek State Park	Waupaca	1962	
Havenwoods State Forest	Milwaukee	1979	
Heritage Hill State Park	Brown	1973	
High Cliff State Park	Calumet	1954	
Hoffman Hills State Recreation Area	Dunn	1980	
Interstate State Park	Polk	1900	
Kettle Moraine State Forest	Washington	1937	
Kinnickinnic State Park	Pierce	1972	
Kohler-Andrae State Park	Sheboygan	1928	
Lake Kegonsa State Park	Dane	1962	
Lake Wissota State Park	Chippewa	1962	
Lakeshore State Park	Milwaukee	1998	
Lost Dauphin State Park	Brown	1947	
Lower Wisconsin State Riverway	Grant, Boundary, Dane	1989	
MacKenzie Center	Columbia	1930	
Menominee River State Recreation Area	Marinette	2010	
Merrick State Park	Buffalo	1932	
Mill Bluff State Park	Monroe, Juneau	1936	
Mirror Lake State Park	Sauk	1962	
Natural Bridge State Park	Sauk	1972	
Nelson Dewey State Park	Grant	1935	
New Glarus Woods State Park	Green	1934	
Newport State Park	Door	1964	
Northern Highland American Legion State Forest	Vilas, Oneida, Iron	1925	
Pattison State Park	Douglas	1920	
Peninsula State Park	Door	1909	
Perrot State Park	Trempealeau	1918	
Point Beach State Forest	Manitowoc	1938	

PARK NAME	COUNTY	EST.	VISITED
Potawatomi State Park	Door	1928	
Rib Mountain State Park	Marathon	1927	
Richard Bong State Recreation Area	Kenosha	1963	
Roche-a-Cri State Park	Adams	1948	
Rock Island State Park	Door	1965	
Rocky Arbor State Park	Juneau	1932	
Sauk Prairie State Recreation Area	Sauk	2004	
Straight Lake State Park	Polk	2002	
Tower Hill State Park	Iowa	1922	
Turtle-Flambeau Scenic Waters Area	Iron	1926	
Whitefish Dunes State Park	Door	1967	
Wildcat Mountain State Park	Vernon	1948	
Willow River State Park	St. Croix	1967	
Wyalusing State Park	Grant	1917	
Yellowstone Lake State Park	Lafayette	1970	

COUNTY	PARK NAME	EST.	VISITED
Adams	Roche-a-Cri State Park	1948	
Ashland	Big Bay State Park	1963	
Ashland	Copper Falls State Park	1929	
Brown	Heritage Hill State Park	1973	
Brown	Lost Dauphin State Park	1947	
Buffalo	Merrick State Park	1932	
Burnett, Polk	Governor Knowles State Forest	1970	
Calumet	High Cliff State Park	1954	
Chippewa	Brunet Island State Park	1936	
Chippewa	Chippewa Moraine State Recreation Area	1971	
Chippewa	Lake Wissota State Park	1962	
Columbia	MacKenzie Center	1930	
Dane	Blue Mound State Park	1959	
Dane	Capital Springs State Recreation Area	2000	
Dane	Cross Plains State Park	1971	
Dane	Governor Nelson State Park	1975	
Dane	Lake Kegonsa State Park	1962	
Door	Newport State Park	1964	
Door	Peninsula State Park	1909	
Door	Potawatomi State Park	1928	
Door	Rock Island State Park	1965	
Door	Whitefish Dunes State Park	1967	
Douglas	Amnicon Falls State Park	1961	
Douglas	Brule River State Forest	1907	
Douglas	Pattison State Park	1920	
Dunn	Hoffman Hills State Recreation Area	1980	
Grant	Nelson Dewey State Park	1935	
Grant	Wyalusing State Park	1917	

COUNTY	PARK NAME	EST.	VISITED
Grant, Boundary, Dane	Lower Wisconsin State Riverway	1989	
Green	Cadiz Springs State Recreation Area	1970	
Green	New Glarus Woods State Park	1934	
Iowa	Governor Dodge State Park	1948	
Iowa	Tower Hill State Park	1922	
Iron	Turtle-Flambeau Scenic Waters Area	1926	
Jackson	Black River State Forest	1957	
Jefferson	Aztalan State Park	1947	
Juneau	Buckhorn State Park	1971	
Juneau	Rocky Arbor State Park	1932	
Kenosha	Richard Bong State Recreation Area	1963	
La Crosse	Coulee Experimental State Forest	1960	
Lafayette	Belmont Mound State Park	1961	
Lafayette	Yellowstone Lake State Park	1970	
Lincoln	Council Grounds State Park	1938	
Maintowoc	Point Beach State Forest	1938	
Manitowoc	Fischer Creek State Recreation Area	1991	
Marathon	Rib Mountain State Park	1927	
Marinette	Governor Thompson State Park	2000	
Marinette	Menominee River State Recreation Area	2010	
Marinette	Governor Earl Peshtigo River State Forest	2001	
Milwaukee	Havenwoods State Forest	1979	
Milwaukee	Lakeshore State Park	1998	
Monroe, Juneau	Mill Bluff State Park	1936	
Oconto	Copper Culture State Park	1959	
Ozaukee	Harrington Beach State Park	1966	
Pierce	Kinnickinnic State Park	1972	
Polk	Interstate State Park	1900	

COUNTY	PARK NAME	EST.	VISITED
Polk	Straight Lake State Park	2002	
Sauk	Devil's Lake State Park	1911	
Sauk	Mirror Lake State Park	1962	
Sauk	Natural Bridge State Park	1972	
Sauk	Sauk Prairie State Recreation Area	2004	
Sawyer	Chippewa Flowage	1923	
Sawyer, Price	Flambeau River State Forest	1930	
Sheboygan	Kohler-Andrae State Park	1928	
St. Croix	Willow River State Park	1967	
Trempealeau	Perrot State Park	1918	
Vernon	Wildcat Mountain State Park	1948	
Vilas, Oneida, Iron	Northern Highland American Legion State Forest	1925	
Walworth	Big Foot Beach State Park	1949	
Washington	Kettle Moraine State Forest	1937	
Waupaca	Hartman Creek State Park	1962	

1 Amnicon Falls State Park
2 Aztalan State Park
3 Belmont Mound State Park
4 Big Bay State Park
5 Big Foot Beach State Park
6 Black River State Forest
7 Blue Mound State Park
8 Brule River State Forest
9 Brunet Island State Park
10 Buckhorn State Park
11 Cadiz Springs State Recreation Area
12 Capital Springs State Recreation Area
13 Chippewa Flowage
14 Chippewa Moraine State Recreation Area
15 Copper Culture State Park
16 Copper Falls State Park
17 Coulee Experimental State Forest
18 Council Grounds State Park
19 Cross Plains State Park
20 Devil's Lake State Park
21 Fischer Creek State Recreation Area
22 Flambeau River State Forest
23 Governor Dodge State Park
24 Governor Earl Peshtigo River State Forest
25 Governor Knowles State Forest
26 Governor Nelson State Park
27 Governor Thompson State Park
28 Harrington Beach State Park
29 Hartman Creek State Park
30 Havenwoods State Forest
31 Heritage Hill State Park
32 High Cliff State Park
33 Hoffman Hills State Recreation Area
34 Interstate State Park
35 Kettle Moraine State Forest
36 Kinnickinnic State Park
37 Kohler-Andrae State Park
38 Lake Kegonsa State Park

39 Lake Wissota State Park
40 Lakeshore State Park
41 Lost Dauphin State Park
42 Lower Wisconsin State Riverway
43 MacKenzie Center
44 Menominee River State Recreation Area
45 Merrick State Park
46 Mill Bluff State Park
47 Mirror Lake State Park
48 Natural Bridge State Park
49 Nelson Dewey State Park
50 New Glarus Woods State Park
51 Newport State Park
52 Northern Highland American Legion State Forest
53 Pattison State Park
54 Peninsula State Park
55 Perrot State Park
56 Point Beach State Forest
57 Potawatomi State Park
58 Rib Mountain State Park
59 Richard Bong State Recreation Area
60 Roche-a-Cri State Park
61 Rock Island State Park
62 Rocky Arbor State Park
63 Sauk Prairie State Recreation Area
64 Straight Lake State Park
65 Tower Hill State Park
66 Turtle-Flambeau Scenic Waters Area
67 Whitefish Dunes State Park
68 Wildcat Mountain State Park
69 Willow River State Park
70 Wyalusing State Park
71 Yellowstone Lake State Park

INVENTORY

- BEAR SPRAY
- BINOCULARS
- CAMERA + ACCESSORIES
- CELL PHONE + CHARGER
- FIRST AID KIT
- FLASHLIGHT/ HEADLAMP
- FLEECE/ WATERPROOF JACKET
- GUIDE BOOK
- HAND LOTION
- HAND SANITIZER
- HIKING SHOES
- INSECT REPELLENT
- LIP BALM
- MEDICATIONS AND PAINKILLERS
- SUNGLASSES
- SNACKS
- SPARE SOCKS
- SUN HAT
- SUNSCREEN
- TOILET PAPER
- TRASH BAGS
- WALKING STICK
- WATER
- WATER SHOES/ SANDALS

AMNICON FALLS STATE PARK

COUNTY: DOUGLAS   **ESTABLISHED:** 1961   **AREA (AC/HA):** 825 / 334

DATE VISITED: **LODGING:**   **WHO I WENT WITH:**

WEATHER: ☼☐ ☁☐ ☷☐ ✳☐ ☂☐ ☁☐   SPRING ☐ SUMMER ☐ FALL ☐ WINTER ☐

FEE(S):   **RATING:** ☆ ☆ ☆ ☆ ☆   **WILL I RETURN?** YES / NO

The park is located in the South Range of Wisconsin, southeast of the town of Superior. It contains a series of waterfalls on the Amnicon River, which flows around a small island and under a historic covered bridge. The waterfalls are divided into upper and lower waterfall areas, and swimming is allowed in both. There are 2.9 miles of trails in the park, which include paths along both banks of the river and a snowshoe trail leading to more remote park areas. Snowshoeing and winter hiking are allowed in the park. There is a 1.5-mile designated snowshoe trail during winter. The park is a place to picnic, camp, hike in the woods, and learn about the Douglas Fault, the geological formation that created the falls. There are three picnic areas along the river by the park office. Picnic tables and grills are also available in the parking area by the covered bridge. Amnicon Falls State Park has 36 camping sites, including one handicapped accessible site and two hiking sites 100 and 150 feet from the parking lot. The campground features swings and a sandbox, as well as a large playground, perfect for family fun. Amnicon Falls State Park offers a quiet, mostly rustic campground, with tall trees partly or fully shading all the sites. The park has 1.8 miles of trails. There are a number of short trails along both sides of the Amnicon River, offering varied views of the falls and surrounding scenery. A 0.8-mile self-guided nature trail provides scenic views of the river as well as access to the river bed downstream from the falls area. Hunting and trapping are allowed in the open areas of the park during the Wisconsin state parks hunting and trapping time frame. The Amnicon River, although better known for its scenic rather than angling qualities, sometimes yields excellent catches. The warm stream flows north into Lake Superior. Below the park, it changes from a fast-flowing river to a slow, wide, and meandering one.

STAMP

AZTALAN STATE PARK

COUNTY: JEFFERSON   **ESTABLISHED:** 1947   **AREA (AC/HA):** 172 / 70

DATE VISITED: **LODGING:**   **WHO I WENT WITH:**

WEATHER: ☀□ ☁□ 🌧□ ❄□ ⛈□ 🌫□   SPRING □ SUMMER □ FALL □ WINTER □

FEE(S):   **RATING:** ☆ ☆ ☆ ☆ ☆   **WILL I RETURN?** YES / NO

The park is a National Historic Landmark and contains one of the most important archaeological sites in the state of Wisconsin. Aztalan is the site of an ancient settlement of the Mississippian culture that flourished from the 10th to 13th centuries. The indigenous people built huge earthen mounds for religious and political purposes. They were part of a widespread culture with important settlements throughout the Mississippi Valley and its tributaries. Their trade network extended from the Great Lakes to the Gulf Coast and Southeast of the present-day United States. Fragments of a palisade and two mounds have been reconstructed in the park. Two miles of trail meander through open prairie and along the Crawfish River. The park is mostly open prairie, with 38 of the 172 acres occupied by oak woodlands. You can kayak, boat, and catch northern pike, catfish, and zander in the Crawfish River. You can picnic in the park, and there is an open shelter with reservations available. Cross-country skiing and snowshoeing are allowed in the winter, but trails are not maintained. Sledding is not permitted at the park. It is illegal to sled on the mounds.

STAMP

BELMONT MOUND STATE PARK

COUNTY: LAFAYETTE **ESTABLISHED:** 1961 **AREA (AC/HA):** 274 / 111

DATE VISITED: **LODGING:** **WHO I WENT WITH:**

WEATHER: ☀☐ ⛅☐ 🌫☐ ❄☐ 🌧☐ 🌊☐ SPRING ☐ SUMMER ☐ FALL ☐ WINTER ☐

FEE(S): **RATING:** ☆ ☆ ☆ ☆ ☆ **WILL I RETURN?** YES / NO

The park includes Belmont Mound, a 1,400-foot hill with a 64-foot high observation tower. The wooded mound is rich in berries and wildlife. "Belmont" comes from the French and means "beautiful mountain." Eighty acres in the northwest corner of the park are designated as Belmont Mound Woods State Natural Area. The park has 2.5 miles of hiking trails. The trails go around the base of the mound, through the center of the park, and to a loop in the northeast corner of the park. The trails are mostly for hiking, but off-road bikes may also use the trails. Belmont Mound State Park provides outdoor recreation opportunities to visitors year-round. Wisconsin's First Capitol historic site is a half mile west of the park. The park is managed by the Belmont Lions Club. Hunting and trapping are allowed in the open areas of the park during the Wisconsin state parks hunting and trapping time frame. Trapping is not permitted in closed areas as noted on the park hunting map or within 100 yards of any designated use area, including trails. There is a picnic area near the park entrance with some playground equipment. The park is open year-round for snowshoeing and winter hiking. Trails are not groomed for skiing.

STAMP

BIG BAY STATE PARK

COUNTY: ASHLAND	ESTABLISHED: 1963	AREA (AC/HA): 2,350 / 951

DATE VISITED: **LODGING:**   **WHO I WENT WITH:**

WEATHER: ☀☐ ☁☐ ☂☐ ☁☐ ⚡☐ 🌬☐   SPRING ☐ SUMMER ☐ FALL ☐ WINTER ☐

FEE(S):   **RATING:** ☆ ☆ ☆ ☆ ☆   **WILL I RETURN?** YES / NO

Located on Madeline Island, the largest of the 22 Apostle Islands in Lake Superior. The park features scenic bluffs, sandstone caves, and a 1.5-mile long sandy beach (a great place for sunbathing). Pets and fires are prohibited on the Big Bay State Park beach. The park does not have a boat launch. Many visitors bring canoes and kayaks to the park and carry them to the beach. From the beach, visitors can paddle around the bay and the lagoon or explore the sea caves around the point. Anglers can catch northern pike in the park's lagoon and several species of trout in Lake Superior. The park is surrounded by unique habitat types and Lakeside dunes, peat bogs, and old-growth forest. Bald eagles return to the park annually to nest and raise their offspring. The park also has a 1-mile boardwalk, hiking trails, a large family campground, and two group camps. Big Bay State Park has a total of 60 campsites. The day-use area is equipped with picnic tables, grills, drinking water, and restrooms. To get to the park, take a ferry from Bayfield to Madeline Island. It contains over 9 miles of trails, including nature trails. Bikes are not allowed on any of the trails or boardwalks. The park is open year-round, although winter visitors are mostly hunters, snow hikers, and cross-country skiers. Bayfield and Madeline Island also offer bus tours, golfing, art galleries, marinas, and the old La Pointe Indian Burial Grounds. Ojibway (Chippewa) Indians were the original inhabitants of the area. Bird watchers are intrigued with the island park. A list of 240 species of birds seen in the park is available at the office. There's a wildlife observation deck along the east shore of the lagoon. Hunting and trapping are allowed in the open areas of the park during the Wisconsin state parks hunting and trapping time frame. Trapping is not permitted in closed areas as noted on the park hunting map or within 100 yards of any designated use area, including trails.

STAMP

BIG FOOT BEACH STATE PARK

COUNTY: WALWORTH   **ESTABLISHED:** 1949   **AREA (AC/HA):** 271 / 110

DATE VISITED: **LODGING:**   **WHO I WENT WITH:**

WEATHER: ☼☐ ☁☐ ☁☐ ❄☐ ⛈☐ 🌬☐   SPRING ☐ SUMMER ☐ FALL ☐ WINTER ☐

FEE(S):   **RATING:** ☆ ☆ ☆ ☆ ☆   **WILL I RETURN?** YES / NO

The park is located on the shores of Lake Geneva. Named for Chief Big Foot of the Potowatomi tribe. The most popular attractions are hiking, swimming, boating, camping, and fishing. Most of the hiking trails are short and have varying levels of difficulty from easy to moderate. Lake Geneva is known for its clear, clean water. Big Foot Beach has a 100-foot marked swimming area. Kayaks and canoes are available in Ceylon Lagoon and Lake Geneva. There are no rental shops in the park, but you can rent equipment from a local vendor south of the park entrance. There is no boat launch in the park. Two public launches are located south of the park, in downtown Lake Geneva and in Linn Township. The north shoreline of the park is a good place to anchor and relax for the day. No lifeguards are on duty. The park offers 5 miles of hiking trails, a family campground, a swimming beach, and picnic and playground areas. Snowshoeing and cross-country skiing are popular in the winter. Big Foot Beach State Park has 100 campsites. Campsites in the upper loop have a gravel pad, fire ring, and picnic table. There are 34 sites with electric pedestals. The campground has a dump station, vault toilets, and a shower building. Firewood, ice, and fire starters can be purchased at the camp host site near the campground entrance.

STAMP

BLACK RIVER STATE FOREST

COUNTY: JACKSON	ESTABLISHED: 1957	AREA (AC/HA): 68,000 / 27,842

DATE VISITED:　　　　**LODGING:**　　　　　**WHO I WENT WITH:**

WEATHER: ☀☐ ☁☐ 🌫☐ ❄☐ 🌧☐ 🌬☐　　SPRING ☐ SUMMER ☐ FALL ☐ WINTER ☐

FEE(S):　　　　**RATING:** ☆ ☆ ☆ ☆ ☆　　　**WILL I RETURN?**　YES / NO

Two forks of the Black River flow through this forest of pine and oak under tall sandstone pillars. Located in the center of the state of Wisconsin property offers many recreational opportunities including camping, kayaking, hunting, hiking, skiing, and ATV riding. Black River State Forest offers 24 miles of trails that meander over and around a very scenic range of hills, cliffs, and bluffs through a mature pine forest. This popular Nordic trail system is considered by many to be among the best in Wisconsin. There are 29 miles of biking trails, five of which are located at the Pigeon Creek campground. At the Black River State Forest, there are many different camping opportunities. Family campgrounds are available at Castle Mound, East Fork, and Pigeon Creek. Group camping is available within the forest. Primitive camping is also available. There are picnic facilities at all three campgrounds (Castle Mound, East Fork, and Pigeon Creek). All have hand pumps for water, picnic tables, grills, and restrooms. Castle Mound and Pigeon Creek have playgrounds and are handicapped accessible. Perry Creek and Oxbow Pond have limited picnic facilities such as picnic tables and grills. The Black River and the East Fork of the Black River offer excellent kayaking opportunities. The East Fork is a scenic river with a gentle current and moderately rocky terrain. Paddling on the East Fork is not recommended when water levels are low. Visitors may even see elk roaming the forest. Elks were released in 2015 and 2016 after more than 125 years of his absence from the area. Access to the forest's lakes, watercourses, and the Black River for fishing is available at many locations. This access is primarily provided by boat launches and fishing piers. Excellent hunting opportunities exist in the Black River State Forest. The forest is open to public hunting during designated seasons with the appropriate license.

STAMP

BLUE MOUND STATE PARK

COUNTY: DANE   **ESTABLISHED:** 1959   **AREA (AC/HA):** 1,153 / 467

DATE VISITED: **LODGING:**   **WHO I WENT WITH:**

WEATHER: ☀☐ ☁☐ ❄☐ ❄☐ 🌧☐ 🌫☐   SPRING ☐ SUMMER ☐ FALL ☐ WINTER ☐

FEE(S):   **RATING:** ☆☆☆☆☆   **WILL I RETURN?** YES / NO

Located atop the highest point in southern Wisconsin, Blue Mound State Park offers spectacular views and unique geological features. The park features a pair of observation towers affording views of the Wisconsin River valley and Baraboo Range to the north, the mounds, buttes, and rolling forests of the Driftless Area to the south and west, and the young glacial plains and city of Madison to the east. More than 20 miles of scenic hiking, off-road biking, and cross-country skiing trails, as well as a family campground, access to the Military Ridge State Trail with bicycle campsites make Blue Mound a popular destination year-round. While all of the trails in the park are open to hiking, there are three trails designated as hiking-only in spring, summer, and fall: the Indian Marker Tree Trail, the self-guided Flintrock Nature Trail, and the Pleasure Valley Hiking Trail. There are 15.5 miles of challenging, off-road singletrack bike trails in the park. A state bicycle card (in addition to a vehicle admission sticker) is required of all bicyclists 16 years of age and older. Trails are open in the spring, summer, and fall unless wet conditions exist. In the winter, trails are closed. The Blue Mound campground is open year-round and offers 77 wooded sites, 12 bike/hike-in sites, and a rustic accessible cabin for people with disabilities. Blue Mound State Park offers a number of beautiful and relaxing opportunities in the picnic area. Play equipment and sandboxes are located in the picnic area near the shelters and in the campground. Next to the picnic area is a nature center with wildlife exhibits. Naturalists offer summer programs. One of the most popular attractions at Blue Mound State Park between Memorial Day and Labor Day is the 1,950-square foot swimming pool and outdoor-themed splash pad. Hunting and trapping are allowed in the open areas of the park during the Wisconsin state parks hunting and trapping time frame. Trapping is not permitted in closed areas as noted on the park hunting map or within 100 yards of any designated use area, including trails. Snowshoeing is allowed anywhere in the park except on cross-country ski trails.

STAMP

BRULE RIVER STATE FOREST

COUNTY: DOUGLAS   **ESTABLISHED:** 1907   **AREA (AC/HA):** 47,000 / 19,020

DATE VISITED: **LODGING:**   **WHO I WENT WITH:**

WEATHER: ☀☐ ☁☐ ⛅☐ ❄☐ ⛈☐ 🌊☐   SPRING ☐ SUMMER ☐ FALL ☐ WINTER ☐

FEE(S):   **RATING:** ☆ ☆ ☆ ☆ ☆   **WILL I RETURN?** YES / NO

The Brule River State Forest offers exceptional recreational opportunities including river paddling, trout fishing, wildlife viewing, a 23-mile stretch of the North Country National Scenic Trail, and 9 miles of Lake Superior shoreline. All 44 miles of the Bois Brule River are in the woods. Two campgrounds offer family camping and access to canoeing on the Bois Brule River. The Bois Brule River in northern Wisconsin offers both a peaceful float with the family and an exciting rapids ride. The Bois Brule River offers easygoing trips on the upper river, particularly from Stones Bridge to Winneboujou that nearly anyone can handle. More adventurous folks can stay on the river another 45 minutes and experience Little Joe Rapids, a modest class II rapids located just upstream of the Bois Brule canoe landing. A canoe rental outfit located in Brule rents out both canoes and kayaks. This business also offers several trips and can pick up or drop off people and canoes. The Bois Brule River is one of Wisconsin's most famous and scenic trout streams. Because of its size, highly productive, self-sustaining fishery, and steady flow of cool spring water, the Brule River is considered one of the best trout streams in the Lake States. All campsites in both Bois Brule and Copper Range campgrounds are reservable. There is the Cedar Island Lodge, "Summer White House" where many American presidents and generals have vacationed. The state forest is popular with kayakers and cross-country skiers. The 1.7-mile loop of the Stoney Hill nature trail begins at Bois Brule Campground. Exhibits showcase the natural and cultural history of the forest. Sections of the trail are steep, but a stop and viewpoint at the top of Stony Hill provide a nice break and a breathtaking view of the Brule River Valley. Pets are not allowed on the nature trail. Horseback riders can enjoy miles of trails within the Brule River State Forest, including the Brule-St. Croix Snowmobile Trail, hiking trails for hunters, and numerous roads. The North Country Trail is for foot traffic only; horses are not allowed on the trail. The Brule River State Forest has more than 40 miles of hunter walking trails that provide easy access to favorable habitat for numerous game animals. Deer and grouse are the most commonly hunted species. Other hunting opportunities include woodcock, bear, and waterfowl.

STAMP

BRUNET ISLAND STATE PARK

COUNTY: CHIPPEWA **ESTABLISHED:** 1936 **AREA (AC/HA):** 1,303 / 496

DATE VISITED: **LODGING:** **WHO I WENT WITH:**

WEATHER: ☀☐ ☁☐ ☷☐ ❄☐ ⛆☐ ☒☐ SPRING ☐ SUMMER ☐ FALL ☐ WINTER ☐

FEE(S): **RATING:** ☆ ☆ ☆ ☆ ☆ **WILL I RETURN?** YES / NO

Quiet lagoons and channels are perfect for canoeing and wildlife watching. The undulating landscape of Chippewa County is a product of the last ice age. The park connects to the Old Abe State Trail, which runs from Cornell to Chippewa Falls. Facilities include 69 campsites, picnic area, electricity, shelters, restrooms, playgrounds, sports field, swimming beach, and hiking trails. Cross-country ski trails are available for winter sports. Vendors in Cornell sell groceries, propane, fuel, and other camping supplies. Laundromats are on Bridge and Main streets. Canoes and kayaks can be rented from a local vendor. Bicycles are allowed on park roads and trails, except for the Jean Brunet Nature Trail. The 2-mile main road through the park includes a designated bicycle and pedestrian lane. Anglers of any age may check out basic fishing equipment free of charge at the park office. You can catch a wide variety of fish including northern pike, walleye, smallmouth bass, catfish, crappie, muskie, and yellow perch. There's an accessible fishing pier near the north camp area and another fishing pier near the south camp area. A Wisconsin fishing license is required. Brunet Island has nearly 20 acres of picnic area available to visitors. The picnic area is on the south and west sides of Brunet Island and offers a scenic view of the Chippewa River and surrounding countryside. A playground and ball diamond are at the southeast end of the picnic area. Hunting and trapping are allowed in the open areas of the park during the Wisconsin state parks hunting and trapping time frame. Trapping is not permitted in closed areas as noted on the park hunting map or within 100 yards of any designated use area, including trails. The island is on a stretch of water extending about 3.5 to 4 miles from the Cornell dam to the Holcombe dam. There is excellent flat water paddling through numerous channels among undeveloped islands in the northern portion of the park.

STAMP

BUCKHORN STATE PARK

COUNTY: JUNEAU   **ESTABLISHED:** 1971   **AREA (AC/HA):** 8,190 / 2,830

DATE VISITED: **LODGING:**   **WHO I WENT WITH:**

WEATHER: ☀☐ ☁☐ ⛆☐ ❄☐ ⛈☐ 🌫☐   SPRING ☐ SUMMER ☐ FALL ☐ WINTER ☐

FEE(S):   **RATING:** ☆ ☆ ☆ ☆ ☆   **WILL I RETURN?** YES / NO

Buckhorn State Park is a paradise for water enthusiasts, hunters, hikers, campers, and nature lovers. Family and group campsites, a canoe trail, and a fishing pier are available within the park. The park occupies a peninsula on Castle Rock Lake, a reservoir formed at the confluence of the Wisconsin and Yellow rivers. The park offers a landscape of sandy soil left by retreating glaciers. There are 7 miles of trails to explore, including one leading to a fish pond for young anglers, a geocaching trail, and one with a 20-foot observation tower. In the winter, five miles of trails are groomed for cross-country skiing. Buckhorn has two picnic areas with grills, tables, water pumps, picnic shelters, and playground equipment. Both shelters can be reserved. In addition, the 1600-acre Buckhorn Wildlife Area and the 2,200-acre Yellow River Wildlife Area next to Buckhorn State Park offers many additional recreation opportunities, including different hunting seasons and access to Castle Rock Flowage. The open waters of the Castle Rock Flowage are the domain of every type of watercraft imaginable. Bass boats, sailboats, ski boats, pontoon boats, jet skis, and even houseboats can be seen in constant motion. The park and wildlife area have five boat ramps. The park has a canoe launch on the peninsula's east side in a quiet slough that leads to the main part of the flowage. Canoe and kayak rentals are available in season from the Friends of Buckhorn State Park and a specially adapted kayak is available for use by people with disabilities. The Castle Rock Flowage channel has earned a reputation as an excellent fishery. The wide variety of fish species found in this watercourse offers anglers year-round action at many locations. The best places to fish from the banks of the Buckhorn include the 90-foot fishing pier at the north picnic area, along the bank at the Buckhorn Bridge, and from the shoreline at the kayak landing. Hunting and trapping are allowed in the open areas of the park during the Wisconsin state parks hunting and trapping time frame. Trapping is not permitted in closed areas as noted on the park hunting map or within 100 yards of any designated use area, including trails. Many winter hikers enjoy skiing the trails, and the relatively flat terrain makes the trails a good place for family outings. When there is enough snow, about 6.5 miles of trails are groomed.

STAMP

CADIZ SPRINGS STATE RECREATION AREA

COUNTY: GREEN   **ESTABLISHED:** 1970   **AREA (AC/HA):** 645 / 261

DATE VISITED: **LODGING:**   **WHO I WENT WITH:**

WEATHER: ☀☐ ☁☐ 🌫☐ ❄☐ ⛈☐ 🌊☐   SPRING ☐ SUMMER ☐ FALL ☐ WINTER ☐

FEE(S):   **RATING:** ☆ ☆ ☆ ☆ ☆   **WILL I RETURN?** YES / NO

Cadiz Springs is a day use area for picnicking, hiking, hunting, fishing, and wildlife viewing. Located in southwestern Wisconsin, the landscape is uniquely different from the rest of the state. The Cadiz Springs State Recreation Area offers visitors a variety of outdoor recreation opportunities throughout the year. The park has 8 miles of hiking trails that offer some of the best places to view a variety of wildlife in natural forest, meadow, and water habitats. The swamps, marshes, and numerous lakes here have been replaced by rolling hills and valleys with spring-fed streams. No camping is allowed at Cadiz Springs. The Cadiz Springs picnic areas offer a variety of grills and picnic tables for day users. The park has two large open shelters with lighting and electricity. Cadiz Springs offers a 150-foot sand beach for swimmers to enjoy. The two lakes in Cadiz Springs have a combined area of 93 acres. There is a boat launch on Beckman Lake. Canoes and kayaks can be taken to Zander Lake. Both Beckman and Zander lakes have restrictions on the use of electric motors only. Fishing is very popular with both warm and cold fish species available. Both lakes have large bass populations and abundant panther populations, providing a pleasant challenge for many anglers who visit these recreational areas. Anglers here can catch brown or rainbow trout, northern pike, catfish, and whitehead. During the winter months, Cadiz Springs State Recreation Area is open to cross-country skiing, although the trails are untracked. Snowshoeing, winter hiking, sledding, and snowmobiling are also allowed in some areas of the park. Hunting and trapping are permitted in the property during legal hunting and trapping seasons.

STAMP

CAPITAL SPRINGS STATE RECREATION AREA

COUNTY: DANE　　　　　　**ESTABLISHED:** 2000　　　　　　**AREA (AC/HA):** 3,000 / 1,200

DATE VISITED:　　　　　**LODGING:**　　　　　**WHO I WENT WITH:**

WEATHER: ☀☐ ☁☐ ☔☐ ❄☐ ⛅☐ 🌊☐　　**SPRING** ☐ **SUMMER** ☐ **FALL** ☐ **WINTER** ☐

FEE(S):　　　　　**RATING:** ☆ ☆ ☆ ☆ ☆　　　　　**WILL I RETURN?** YES / NO

Just minutes from downtown Madison, Capital Springs State Recreation Area and Lake Farm Park in Dane County offers many recreational opportunities including camping, hiking and skiing trails, picnicking, fishing, and boat launching on Lake Waubesa. There are several large picnic areas and playgrounds near Lake Waubesa. Three shelters can be reserved. Recreational opportunities include wildlife viewing, cross-country skiing, snowshoeing, canoeing, and hunting. During winter, 6 miles of trails are groomed for cross-country skiing. The boat launch is open year-round. Each vehicle parked in the boat launch parking area must have a lake access permit. Fishing is available in Lake Waubesa. Fishing licenses are required. Dane County's Lake Farm Park, adjacent to Capital Springs, offers camping. There are over 6 miles of hiking trails and walking paths in Capital Springs. Some trails have interpretive signs along the way to help hikers learn more about the area. Due to the variety of natural habitats, there is excellent bird watching throughout the year. The Capital Springs State Trail winds through the Capital Springs State Recreation Area. Direct access to the trail is at the campground in Lake Farm County Park near the Lussier Family Heritage Center. This paved trail is popular with cyclists and connects to several other Madison city and state trails. There are many parks, trails, and natural resource points of interest along the border of the Capital Springs Recreation Area. Hunting and trapping are allowed in the open areas of the park during the Wisconsin state parks hunting and trapping time frame.

STAMP

CHIPPEWA FLOWAGE

COUNTY: SAWYER   **ESTABLISHED:** 1923   **AREA (AC/HA):** 15,300 / 6,197

DATE VISITED: **LODGING:**   **WHO I WENT WITH:**

WEATHER: ☀☐ ☁☐ ☔☐ ❄☐ ⛈☐ 🌬☐   SPRING ☐ SUMMER ☐ FALL ☐ WINTER ☐

FEE(S):   **RATING:** ☆ ☆ ☆ ☆ ☆   **WILL I RETURN?** YES / NO

The damming of the Chippewa River joined the waters of 11 natural lakes, 9 rivers, and countless streams. Six boat access sites provide public access to the Chippewa Flowage; four provided by the DNR, one provided by the Lac Courte Oreilles Tribe (LCO), and one provided by the Town of Hayward. Boaters should be aware of changing canal conditions, especially fluctuating water levels, and exercise caution at all times. At the water's edge, you may see deer, bears, herons, otters, eagles, beavers, and even elk. The Chippewa Flowage provides a unique Northwoods fishery with a wide variety of species. Walleye, northern pike, large and smallmouth bass, crappie, bluegill, and perch are abundant. This is the ideal place to enjoy quiet sports like kayaking, canoeing, bird watching, hiking, and cross country skiing. There are about a dozen golf courses in this area. There are 18 primitive camping sites on the island, available for public use. Some are available on a first-come, first-served basis, and some are available by reservation. Each public campground is marked with a sign and has a fire pit, picnic table, and outdoor latrine. Camping is allowed only in designated campgrounds. All campsites are accessible by water only. Campsites may be closed or relocated to allow for vegetation regeneration and/or to protect threatened, endangered, or sensitive species and their habitats. Campsites are also available at private resorts in the area. There are 2 miles of hiking and ski trails on DNR land on the north side of the flowage that can be accessed via a parking area adjacent to County Highway B between Moss Creek and Hay Creek.

STAMP

CHIPPEWA MORAINE STATE RECREATION AREA

COUNTY: CHIPPEWA   **ESTABLISHED:** 1971   **AREA (AC/HA):** 3,568 / 1,324

DATE VISITED: **LODGING:**   **WHO I WENT WITH:**

WEATHER: ☀□ ☁□ ☁□ ❄□ ⚡□ 🌫□   SPRING ☐ SUMMER ☐ FALL ☐ WINTER ☐

FEE(S):   **RATING:** ☆ ☆ ☆ ☆ ☆   **WILL I RETURN?** YES / NO

The Chippewa Moraine State Recreation Area, located along the Ice Age National Scenic Trail, offers unspoiled beauty with kettle lakes and many glacial features. The Ice Age National Scenic Trail travels through the Chippewa Moraine, connecting to the interpretive center and loop trails and the three primitive, outpost campsites. The entire trail is over 1,000 miles long and follows the edge of the last continental glacier in Wisconsin. Most of the woods are mature maple/pine. The Chippewa Moraine segment of the Ice Age National Scientific Reserve includes 23 miles of trails. The trails are for hikers only, and motorized vehicles, horses, or mountain bikes are not allowed on the Chippewa Moraine. Trails are well laid out and provide many options. Hiking, snowshoeing, backpacking, fishing, and bird watching are popular activities. Whether you choose to hike in warmer weather or snowshoe in winter, there is always fun to be had on the many trails with optional distances. Snow gives you the ability to move around in snowshoes, allowing you to go places you can't go without snow. North and South Shattuck, Jeanstow, Knickerbocker, Townline, Horseshoe, and Plummer lakes offer boating, canoeing, and kayaking opportunities. Fishing is available in the many lakes within the Chippewa Moraine. The David R. Obey Ice Age Interpretive Center offers first-class exhibits on glacial, cultural, and natural history. There is a larger room for group presentations and indoor and outdoor seating to enjoy the views to the south and west. There are picnic tables outside the interpretive center. Here you will find a return to nature. It's a great place for the whole family. Hunting and trapping are permitted in the property during legal hunting and trapping seasons. No person may hunt or trap without first obtaining a property map identifying those areas closed to hunting and trapping within the property.

STAMP

COPPER CULTURE STATE PARK

COUNTY: OCONTO   **ESTABLISHED:** 1959   **AREA (AC/HA):** 42 / 17

DATE VISITED: **LODGING:**   **WHO I WENT WITH:**

WEATHER: ☼☐ ☁☐ ☷☐ ❄☐ ☔☐ ☁☐   SPRING ☐ SUMMER ☐ FALL ☐ WINTER ☐

FEE(S):   **RATING:** ☆ ☆ ☆ ☆ ☆   **WILL I RETURN?** YES / NO

Copper Culture State Park was the site of a prehistoric cemetery of the Old Copper Complex people who occupied the northern Midwest from ca. 4000 – 2000 BC. It was rediscovered in 1952 by a 13-year-old boy who discovered human bones while playing in an old quarry. The 42-acre park is just west of the city of Oconto. Visitors can walk throughout the park and along the Oconto River, or tour the museum with artifacts end exhibits detailing the importance of the property. There is a nice hiking trail to the river that has some signage about the historical significance of the area. On the Oconto River, you can fish from the shore. The park and museum are operated by the Oconto County Historical Society. The park is very peaceful and well maintained. It is a good idea to bring insect spray with you.

STAMP

COPPER FALLS STATE PARK

COUNTY: ASHLAND   **ESTABLISHED:** 1929   **AREA (AC/HA):** 3,068 / 1,242

DATE VISITED: **LODGING:**   **WHO I WENT WITH:**

WEATHER: ☀☐ ☁☐ ☷☐ ❄☐ ⛈☐ 🌬☐   SPRING ☐ SUMMER ☐ FALL ☐ WINTER ☐

FEE(S):   **RATING:** ☆ ☆ ☆ ☆ ☆   **WILL I RETURN?** YES / NO

Ancient lava flows, deep gorges, and spectacular waterfalls make Copper Falls State Park one of Wisconsin's most scenic parks. Log buildings built by the Civilian Conservation Corps in the 1930s add to the park's charm. The park offers camping, hiking, bicycling, picnicking, fishing, and swimming opportunities in Loon Lake. The 1.7-mile Doughboy's Nature Trail, along the Bad River, is one of the best hikes in Wisconsin. There are 17 miles of trails in the park, including part of the North Country National Scenic Trail. The trails are designed for hiking, biking, cross-country skiing, and snowshoeing. The park offers winter camping and ice fishing on Loon Lake. Copper Falls has two one-way mountain bike trails that are open to cyclists and hikers when not covered in snow. The Vahterra Trail runs east of the parking lot at Ballfield, and the Takesson Trail runs south of North Campground. Bicycling is only allowed on designated bike trails and park roads. There is a 300-foot sandy beach for swimming at Loon Lake. The beach has a paved path leading to the water's edge. There are no lifeguards. Copper Falls State Park features small carry-in boat access on Loon Lake for canoes and kayaks. Several other lakes within 10 miles of the park offer boat launch facilities and opportunities for larger watercraft. Copper Falls State Park has two campgrounds with shaded and wooded sites well separated from popular public use areas to provide campers with a sense of seclusion. Copper Falls is located in the heart of an excellent fishing area, with numerous lakes offering all types of sport fishing within a short drive. Visitors can catch largemouth bass, northern pike, and panfish in Loon Lake. The main picnic area at Copper Falls State Park, on the banks of the Bad River, is over 5 acres. It features several picnic tables and grills, a spacious log shelter, a concession stand, and a playground. The picnic area is located at the beginning of the Doughboys Nature Trail, which leads to Copper and Brownstone Falls. Hunting and trapping are allowed in the open areas of the park during the Wisconsin state parks hunting and trapping time frame.

STAMP

COULEE EXPERIMENTAL STATE FOREST

COUNTY: LA CROSSE   **ESTABLISHED:** 1960   **AREA (AC/HA):** 2,944 / 1,191

DATE VISITED: **LODGING:**   **WHO I WENT WITH:**

WEATHER: ☀☐ ⛅☐ 🌫☐ ❄☐ 🌩☐ 🌧☐   SPRING ☐ SUMMER ☐ FALL ☐ WINTER ☐

FEE(S):   **RATING:** ☆ ☆ ☆ ☆ ☆   **WILL I RETURN?** YES / NO

The Coulee State Experimental Forest is a unique property in the state of Wisconsin. This forest is used for long-term forest watershed research to develop land management practices. Coulee describes the area accurately as the forest has many deep ravines and gullies. The property is managed for forest production and wildlife habitat and offers recreational opportunities for hunting, cross-country skiing, hiking, and horseback riding. Horseback riding is prohibited in Native Community Management Areas, on the ski trails when snow-covered, and on any trail in the spring when the ground is soft. The 12-mile ski trail can be used for hiking when not covered by snow. Primitive forest roads are also open for many forms of recreation, snowshoeing, wildlife viewing, and nature study. The Coulee Experimental State Forest provides one of the few large, public upland forests in La Crosse County suitable for hunting a variety of species. Primary game species include deer, ruffed grouse, squirrels, turkeys, and rabbits.

STAMP

COUNCIL GROUNDS STATE PARK

COUNTY: LINCOLN   **ESTABLISHED:** 1938   **AREA (AC/HA):** 509 / 206

DATE VISITED: **LODGING:**   **WHO I WENT WITH:**

WEATHER: ☀☐ ☁☐ 🌧☐ ❄☐ ⛈☐ 🌫☐   SPRING ☐ SUMMER ☐ FALL ☐ WINTER ☐

FEE(S):   **RATING:** ☆ ☆ ☆ ☆ ☆   **WILL I RETURN?** YES / NO

Located on the beautiful Wisconsin River near Native American encampments, Council Grounds State Park is a favorite of water enthusiasts. The park offers many recreational opportunities, including family and group campsites, forest trails, a beach, and an accessible fishing pier. The 217-foot-long beach has an extensive sunbathing area and picnic area. The best time to swim is mid-June and mid-August. There are no lifeguards here. Boating and water skiing are popular on the lake. The park has a boat landing near the accessible fishing pier and beach. The boat landing provides access to Lake Alexander and the Wisconsin River. The Friends of Council Grounds State Park rent canoes and kayaks in season. Council Grounds State Park offers family and group campsites. A large picnic area is located near the beach at Alexander Lake. Picnic areas are also located near the Big Pines Nature Trail and the refuge building. An accessible fishing pier is on the northwest side of the park near the boat landing. Common fish species in Lake Alexander include northern pike, walleye, smallmouth bass, muskies, yellow perch, bluegills, and black crappies. Several trails run through different parts of the park, offering hikers flat or rolling terrain. The 2.5-mile main road in the park is also popular with walkers and joggers. Originally a Merrill city park, it was donated to the state in 1938, evolving from a state roadside park into a state forest to full state park status in 1978. Hunting and trapping are allowed in the open areas of the park during the Wisconsin state parks hunting and trapping time frame. Cross-country skiing and snowshoeing are available in the winter.

STAMP

CROSS PLAINS STATE PARK

COUNTY: DANE   **ESTABLISHED:** 1971   **AREA (AC/HA):** 1,500 / 610

DATE VISITED: **LODGING:**   **WHO I WENT WITH:**

WEATHER: ☼☐ ☁☐ ☷☐ ❄☐ ⛆☐ ☋☐   SPRING ☐ SUMMER ☐ FALL ☐ WINTER ☐

FEE(S):   **RATING:** ☆ ☆ ☆ ☆ ☆   **WILL I RETURN?** YES / NO

The Ice Age Complex at Cross Plains is a part of the National Ice Age Scientific Reserve. Located just west of Madison near the village of Cross Plains, this area contains an outstanding collection of glacial landforms, a gorge carved by meltwater, and expansive views of both driftless and glaciated terrain. Fishing is available at Shoveler's Sink, on land owned by the U.S. Fish and Wildlife Service. Anglers 16 years of age and older must have a Wisconsin fishing license. All federal, state and county lands are open to hikers and walkers year-round. Some hiking trails are located on DNR lands north of Old Sauk Pass Road and on National Park Service lands. Hunting and trapping are allowed in the open areas of the DNR land south and west of Old Sauk Pass Road during the Wisconsin state parks hunting and trapping time frame. In winter, you can enjoy cross-country skiing, snowshoeing, and hiking.

STAMP

DEVIL'S LAKE STATE PARK

COUNTY: SAUK | **ESTABLISHED:** 1911 | **AREA (AC/HA):** 10,200 / 4,100

DATE VISITED: | **LODGING:** | **WHO I WENT WITH:**

WEATHER: ☀☐ ☁☐ 🌧☐ ❄☐ ⛈☐ 🌫☐ | SPRING ☐ SUMMER ☐ FALL ☐ WINTER ☐

FEE(S): | **RATING:** ☆ ☆ ☆ ☆ ☆ | **WILL I RETURN?** YES / NO

Devil's Lake State Park, located along the Ice Age National Scenic Trail, offers stunning views from 500-foot quartzite bluffs overlooking the 360-acre lake. Devil's Lake State Park offers many outdoor recreational opportunities that visitors can enjoy throughout the year. Visitors can enjoy nearly 30 miles of hiking trails, lakeside picnic areas, swimming beaches, paddling areas, and year-round nature programs. The park has 1.5 miles of trail that are accessible for people with disabilities. Trails are not maintained for winter use but are not closed. In addition to skiing, snowshoeing and ice fishing, visitors also enjoy dog sledding, building igloos, geocaching, and orienteering courses. The park has four miles of off-road bike trails-the Upland Trail Loop. Two free boat launches are available in the park: on the north shore near the castle and along Park Road between the north and south shores. There are two beaches, one at each end of the lake, totaling 3,300 feet in length. Each beach has a bathhouse. Lifeguards are not provided. Scuba diving is popular at the park. Diving flags are required. Many anglers come to the park to fish from the lakeshore or from boats (electric motor only). The lake is home to brook trout, walleye, northern pike, bass, and panfish. Ice fishing is popular at Devil's Lake. In winter, savvy anglers catch brown trout, northern pike, and other fish. There are large picnic areas on both the north and south shores of Devil's Lake. Each area has tables, drinking water (in season), and grills. Devil's Lake State Park has three regular campgrounds with 423 sites for families of one to six people. There are also nine group campsites that can accommodate a total of 240 people. All campgrounds are available for reservations. There are many quartzite rock formations throughout the park, such as Balanced Rock and Devil's Doorway. Hunting and trapping are allowed in the open areas of the park during the Wisconsin state parks hunting and trapping time frame.

STAMP

FISCHER CREEK STATE RECREATION AREA

COUNTY: MANITOWOC   **ESTABLISHED:** 1991   **AREA (AC/HA):** 142 / 57

DATE VISITED: **LODGING:**   **WHO I WENT WITH:**

WEATHER: ☀️☐ ⛅☐ 🌧️☐ ❄️☐ ☁️☐ 🌬️☐   SPRING ☐ SUMMER ☐ FALL ☐ WINTER ☐

FEE(S):   **RATING:** ☆ ☆ ☆ ☆ ☆   **WILL I RETURN?** YES / NO

Fischer Creek has about one mile of Lake Michigan shoreline, scenic wooded bluffs, meadows, and wetlands. It's a place for hiking, picnicking, wildlife viewing, and relaxing on the beach. The tract is a mixture of young forest, marsh, and grassland crossed by the creek, a Class II trout stream with spring and fall runs of fish from Lake Michigan. This is a beautiful area for enjoying peaceful and quiet time. There are two parking lots here, separated by Fischer Creek.

STAMP

FLAMBEAU RIVER STATE FOREST

COUNTY: SAWYER, PRICE   **ESTABLISHED:** 1930   **AREA (AC/HA):** 90,147 / 36,481

DATE VISITED: **LODGING:**   **WHO I WENT WITH:**

WEATHER: ☀☐ ☁☐ 🌧☐ ❄☐ ⛅☐ 🌫☐   SPRING ☐ SUMMER ☐ FALL ☐ WINTER ☐

FEE(S):   **RATING:** ☆ ☆ ☆ ☆ ☆   **WILL I RETURN?** YES / NO

The Flambeau River State Forest provides excellent backcountry opportunities, including wooded hiking trails, ATV and snowmobile trails, family campgrounds and rustic river sites, hunting, and fishing. Canoeing is the most popular activity in the forest. Different portions of the river offer varying degrees of difficulty. The North Fork is ideal for the novice, while the South Fork is for the advanced paddler. Nine landings offer access to forest lakes and the Flambeau River. The forest is composed of northern hardwoods. The Flambeau River State Forest has 38 miles of ATV trails. The trails are usually open from May 15 to November 15. When riding in the forest, stick to the designated trails. The 14-mile Flambeau Hills Ski trail is open to cyclists in the summer. Flambeau River State Forest offers two family campgrounds with reservable sites. Access to forested lakes and the Flambeau River provides many places to fish. This access is primarily provided by boat launches and fishing piers. There are many opportunities for hiking in the forest. Nature trails without interpretive signs can be found at both the Connors Lake Campground and Lake of the Pines Campground. Hiking is allowed on the Flambeau Hills Ski Trail during summer, and in winter whenever the trails are not groomed for cross-country skiing. In winter when trails are not groomed for cross-country skiing, visitors may snowshoe or hike. Excellent hunting conditions exist in the national forests. Picnic facilities with drinking water, flush toilets, picnic tables, grills, and playground equipment are located at Connors Lake along W Highway.

STAMP

GOVERNOR DODGE STATE PARK

COUNTY: IOWA   **ESTABLISHED:** 1948   **AREA (AC/HA):** 5,350 / 2,130

DATE VISITED: **LODGING:**   **WHO I WENT WITH:**

WEATHER: ☀☐ ⛅☐ 🌫☐ ❄☐ ☁☐ 🌧☐   SPRING ☐ SUMMER ☐ FALL ☐ WINTER ☐

FEE(S):   **RATING:** ☆ ☆ ☆ ☆ ☆   **WILL I RETURN?** YES / NO

Governor Dodge State Park includes steep hills, bluffs, and deep valleys plus two lakes and a waterfall. Located in Wisconsin's scenic driftless area, Governor Dodge offers camping, picnicking, hiking, canoeing, biking, hunting, fishing, off-road biking, cross-country skiing, and horseback riding opportunities. Popular activities include also boating, and swimming on the park's two lakes. Named after Henry Dodge, the first governor of the Wisconsin Territory, the park contains geologic features indicative of the Driftless Area. In the park, various species of animals, such as white-tailed deer, shrew, wild turkey, black grouse, beaver, red fox, and gray fox. There are 8 miles of challenging off-road bike trails in the park. A State Trail Pass is required to use the bike trails. There are swimming beaches on both lakes. The swimming areas are located near both beaches. There are launch ramps on both Cox Hollow and Twin Valley lakes. Paddleboats and kayaks can be rented daily from Memorial Day Weekend through Labor Day at the concession stand on Cox Hollow Beach. Rentals are also available on spring and fall weekends. The lakes in the park offer excellent fishing. Fish species such as bass, walleye, muskie, and panfish are found here. Fishing licenses are required and can be purchased at local bait stores. Governor Dodge State Park has more than 300 camping sites, ranging from standard and group camping to equestrian camping and remote backpacking sites. Governor Dodge maintains nearly 40 miles of trails. All are open to hikers, except for the ski trails when they are covered in snow. The park has 22 miles of bridle trails providing riders an unequaled view of Governor Dodge's rich and varied landscape. Hunting and trapping are allowed in the open areas of the park during the Wisconsin state parks hunting and trapping time frame. There are eight designated picnic sites. Picnic shelters are available at Enee Point, the amphitheater, the Twin Valley Picnic Area, and at Cox Hollow and Twin Valley beaches.

STAMP

GOVERNOR EARL PESHTIGO RIVER STATE FOREST

COUNTY: MARINETTE	ESTABLISHED: 2001	AREA (AC/HA): 12,400 / 5,018

DATE VISITED:　　　　**LODGING:**　　　　**WHO I WENT WITH:**

WEATHER: ☀☐ ☁☐ 🌫☐ ❄☐ 🌦☐ 🌬☐　　SPRING ☐ SUMMER ☐ FALL ☐ WINTER ☐

FEE(S):　　　　**RATING:** ☆ ☆ ☆ ☆ ☆　　**WILL I RETURN?** YES / NO

The forest is on the Peshtigo River and is next to Governor Thompson State Park. It is a long, linear state forest in northeast Wisconsin bordering some of the most beautiful and exciting sections of the Peshtigo River. Anglers know the river's free-flowing portion for its excellent fly-fishing, and paddlers brave the Midwest's longest continuous whitewater rapids. More than 3,200 acres of water in the Governor Earl Peshtigo River State Forest offer scenic boating and paddling opportunities, as well as access to the islands and backwaters of the Peshtigo River. The state forest has two beaches for visitors to enjoy. Old Veteran's Lake Beach offers 10 acres of exceptionally clear water and a small beach for enjoyment. The forest offers a family campground and several remote boat-in campsites along the river. A small portion of the Woodland ATV Trail runs through the state forest. Other than snowmobile trails that ATVs can use in the winter, this is the only place in the state forest accessible to ATVs. There are two trail systems on the national forest. Numerous roads and volunteer-maintained hiking trails for hunters are also available for hikers. There are no designated equestrian trails or mountain bike trails on the state forest, but the forest is open to these activities. Except during the winter months, snowmobile trails and angler access roads are open to horseback riders and mountain bikers. The Governor Earl Peshtigo River State Forest offers ample opportunities for hunters and trappers seeking all types of game. The majority of lands within the state forest are open to hunting during the scheduled seasons. White-tail deer, small game, black bear, and migratory birds are the primary game species. Trappers can find beaver, muskrat, raccoon, fisher, and mink on the property.

STAMP

GOVERNOR KNOWLES STATE FOREST

COUNTY: BURNETT, POLK **ESTABLISHED:** 1970 **AREA (AC/HA):** 19,753 / 7,993

DATE VISITED: **LODGING:** **WHO I WENT WITH:**

WEATHER: ☀☐ ⛅☐ 🌧☐ ❄☐ ☁☐ 🌬☐ SPRING ☐ SUMMER ☐ FALL ☐ WINTER ☐

FEE(S): **RATING:** ☆ ☆ ☆ ☆ ☆ **WILL I RETURN?** YES / NO

On the east the state forest is bordered by county forests and two state wildlife areas. Originally called the St. Croix River State Forest, it was renamed in 1981 to honor former Wisconsin governor Warren P. Knowles for his conservation and outdoorsman ethics. This 55-mile-long forest in northwestern Wisconsin parallels the St. Croix National Scenic Riverway and offers camping, paddling, hiking, horseback riding, biking, hunting, fishing, cross-country skiing, and snowmobiling opportunities. Bicycles are allowed on all trails except those marked as closed. Trails are unpaved, off-road, and vary in difficulty. Governor Knowles State Forest offers nine primitive campsites along the hiking trails. You can canoe or kayak the Wood River from Grantsburg to Raspberry Landing on the St. Croix River. The St. Croix River meanders through wild and scenic terrain, with its source in the spruce-fir swamps near Upper St. Croix Lake. Governor Knowles State Forest has a total of 40 miles of hiking trails that stretch through the wild and scenic valley of the St. John River. This trail system is divided into two segments. The northern segment is 23 miles long and the southern segment is 17 miles long. Hunters will find deer, turkey, black bear, squirrels, grouse, and woodcock.

STAMP

GOVERNOR NELSON STATE PARK

COUNTY: DANE		ESTABLISHED: 1975		AREA (AC/HA): 422 / 171

DATE VISITED:	LODGING:		WHO I WENT WITH:	

WEATHER: ☀☐ ☁☐ ☂☐ ❄☐ ⛆☐ ⛅☐ SPRING ☐ SUMMER ☐ FALL ☐ WINTER ☐

FEE(S):	RATING: ☆ ☆ ☆ ☆ ☆	WILL I RETURN? YES / NO

It was named in honor of former Governor of the State of Wisconsin, Gaylord Nelson. Governor Nelson is a day use park offering a sand beach, boat launch, fish cleaning facility, picnic areas and playground equipment, prairie restorations, and over 8 miles of trails. Away from the lake, one can find restored prairie and savanna, effigy mounds, hiking trails, and ski trails. Native American effigy mounds can be seen on the Woodland Trail. The park has a four-stall boat launch. Game fish and panfish are plentiful in Lake Mendota, allowing for year-round fishing. An accessible fishing pier next to the boat landing provides visitors with a great place to fish or just relax and enjoy the feel of the lake. During spring, summer, and fall, you can hike 8.4 miles of trails through a wide variety of ecological communities, including oak woodlands and savannas. Wildflowers bloom abundantly along the trails, and a variety of animals can often be spotted while hiking. There are also two accessible viewing platforms with information boards along the trails. Grills are located in the picnic area. Campfires are not allowed in the park. You can reserve two shelters on the beach and in the picnic area. In the winter, trails are laid out for sloping skiers and groomed for skaters. Most of them are easy or moderately difficult.

STAMP

GOVERNOR THOMPSON STATE PARK

COUNTY: MARINETTE   **ESTABLISHED:** 2000   **AREA (AC/HA):** 2,800 / 1,100

DATE VISITED: **LODGING:**   **WHO I WENT WITH:**

WEATHER: ☀☐ ☁☐ ☔☐ ❄☐ ⛅☐ 🌫☐   SPRING ☐ SUMMER ☐ FALL ☐ WINTER ☐

FEE(S):   **RATING:** ☆ ☆ ☆ ☆ ☆   **WILL I RETURN?** YES / NO

Governor Thompson State Park is a scenic forested park near Crivitz, Wisconsin. The park contains 6.5 miles of shoreline on the Caldron Falls Reservoir, part of the Peshtigo River, and 5,300 feet of shoreline on two small kettle lakes. Adjacent lands are part of the Peshtigo River State Forest. The park has hiking trails where you can observe all kinds of wild animals, from the black grouse and turkey to wild deer, or visit the off-season to take advantage of the cross-country skiing trail that is maintained during the winter months. Governor Thompson State Park has over 16 miles of hiking trails. There is a popular boat launch on the Caldron Falls Reservoir, South Bay, or Boat Landing #13. The launch facilities include two concrete launches, a boarding dock, a fishing pier, a paved parking lot, a picnic area, and restrooms. Woods Lake has a 150-foot sandy beach for swimming, a grassy sunbathing area, and a restroom with changing facilities. Governor Thompson State Park has a family campground and three boat sites. Fishing is available to those who enjoy a quiet experience. The most popular fish are bluegills, crappies, northern, and bass. The Woods Lake area has picnic tables and benches. Hunting and trapping are allowed in the open areas of the park during the Wisconsin state parks hunting and trapping time frame. In the winter, trails are tracked for diagonal skiers and groomed for skate skiers.

STAMP

HARRINGTON BEACH STATE PARK

COUNTY: OZAUKEE   **ESTABLISHED:** 1966   **AREA (AC/HA):** 715 / 258

DATE VISITED: **LODGING:**   **WHO I WENT WITH:**

WEATHER: ☀☐ ⛅☐ 🌧☐ ❄☐ ⛈☐ 🌬☐   SPRING ☐ SUMMER ☐ FALL ☐ WINTER ☐

FEE(S):   **RATING:** ☆ ☆ ☆ ☆ ☆   **WILL I RETURN?** YES / NO

Harrington Beach State Park has more than a mile of beach along Lake Michigan. This park also features a white cedar and hardwood swamp, old field grasslands with restored wetland ponds, and a scenic limestone quarry lake. Camp, sunbathe, picnic, hike, bird watch, fish, or practice astronomy at one of the observatory's monthly public viewings. From the 1890s until 1925, a dolomite quarry operated on the site of the park. At Harrington Beach State Park, the Quarry Lake Trail is accessible for wheelchairs. Biking is allowed on the shuttle bus route from the Pucket's Pond area to the Ansay Welcome Center. There is no boat launch in the park. Users of small craft or watercraft should be aware of wind conditions on Lake Michigan. Swimming and boating are not permitted in Quarry Lake or Puckett's Pond. Harrington Beach State Park has a family campground, with five walk-in sites, a group campsite, an accessible cabin for people with disabilities, and a kayak site. Surf fishing for salmon and trout draws visitors to Harrington Beach and Lake Michigan. Anglers can also fish from the shore of the 26-acre Quarry Lake and Puckett's Pond. Trout, crappie, bluegill, and other fish can be caught there. Harrington Beach State Park has seven miles of hiking trails. Walking the beach along Lake Michigan, hikers can see the remains of a 700-foot pier that was used in the early 1900s for shipping limestone quarried and processed at the park. The old pier is on the point which is the dividing point between the north and south beaches. Beautiful views of Lake Michigan extend from picnic areas in the south of the park. Reservation shelters are available in these areas and at the Puckett's Pond picnic area by the upper parking lot. Sand volleyball courts are also available in the park. Hunting and trapping are allowed in the open areas of the park during the Wisconsin state parks hunting and trapping time frame. A cross-country ski trail runs from the lower parking lot along the shuttle bus route to the Hardwood Swamp trail, then back east along the service road. A snowmobile trail runs through the west end of the park.

STAMP

HARTMAN CREEK STATE PARK

COUNTY: WAUPACA   **ESTABLISHED:** 1966   **AREA (AC/HA):** 1,500 / 573

DATE VISITED: **LODGING:**   **WHO I WENT WITH:**

WEATHER: ☀☐ ⛅☐ 🌫☐ ❄☐ 🌧☐ 🌊☐   SPRING ☐ SUMMER ☐ FALL ☐ WINTER ☐

FEE(S):   **RATING:** ☆ ☆ ☆ ☆ ☆   **WILL I RETURN?** YES / NO

Located on the beautiful Chain O' Lakes, Hartman Creek State Park is a quiet and friendly, natural gem and a popular destination in central Wisconsin. The park offers camping, boating, swimming, horseback riding, and mountain biking opportunities, the historic Hellestad House log cabin, and picnic areas including Whispering Pines along Marl Lake. Seven lakes with crystal clear waters, a sandy swimming beach, and miles of different types of trails make summer an excellent time to visit the park. Hikers have about 10 miles of varied trails to choose from at Hartman Creek State Park. Before being established as a state park in 1966, Hartman Creek was a fish hatchery, where dams were built to create four spring-fed lakes - Allen, Hartman, Grebe, and Middle. The park is located on part of the terminal moraine of the Wisconsin glacier, and potholes, gullies, and springs feed the lakes. The Ice Age National Scenic Trail passes through the park. There are about 12 miles of off-road biking trails in the park which are combination hiking/biking segments. Hartman Lake has a 300-foot sand beach and large marked-off swimming area. The beach is adjacent to 3 acres of multi-use lawn area containing picnic tables, drinking water, and a combination of changing and toilet building. Paddlers can launch canoes or kayaks from the boat landing off Knight Lane on Manomin Lake and paddle through the east end of Hartman Creek State Park and the Pope Lake Natural Area to Marl Lake. From the floating dock at Marl Lake, a stone staircase leads to the Whispering Pines picnic area where paddlers can break for lunch. The picnic area has tables, grills, bathrooms, drinking water and a vehicle access point, and a parking lot off of Whispering Pines Road. Hartman Creek State Park has a 103-site family campground and five group camping sites. The lakes have largemouth bass, perch, bluegill, and other panfish. Fishing piers, accessible to persons with disabilities, are along the east shore of Allen Lake and at Whispering Pines on Marl Lake. There are four picnic areas with tables, benches, grills, drinking water, and parking. Hunting and trapping are allowed in the open areas of the park during the Wisconsin state parks hunting and trapping time frame.

STAMP

HAVENWOODS STATE FOREST

COUNTY: MILWAUKEE   **ESTABLISHED:** 1979   **AREA (AC/HA):** 237 / 95,9

DATE VISITED: **LODGING:**   **WHO I WENT WITH:**

WEATHER: ☀☐ ⛅☐ 🌫☐ ❄☐ 🌧☐ 🌬☐   SPRING ☐ SUMMER ☐ FALL ☐ WINTER ☐

FEE(S):   **RATING:** ☆ ☆ ☆ ☆ ☆   **WILL I RETURN?** YES / NO

The forest was created to provide an urban green space and environmental education center. The land includes grasslands, woods, wetlands, Lincoln Creek, an urban arboretum, and education gardens. The Environmental Awareness Center includes an auditorium, classrooms, displays, and a resource center. There are trails for nature study, hiking, biking, and cross-country skiing. Schoenecker Park abuts the property on the northeast. Limestone trails and paved roads (approximately 2 miles) are accessible by bicycle. Use caution as these trails are shared with hikers. More than 6 miles of trails encourage hikers, runners, and joggers to explore the woods, wetlands, and meadows on the property. With several different sections of trails, visitors can choose routes of varying lengths. Visitors may picnic anywhere in the forest. Picnic tables are located in the Urban Arboretum and by the parking lot. No campfires or barbecues are allowed. Cross-country skiers are welcome in the woods. The trails are not groomed. The terrain at Havenwoods is mostly flat, making it a good place for beginner skiers.

STAMP

HERITAGE HILL STATE PARK

COUNTY: BROWN   **ESTABLISHED:** 1973   **AREA (AC/HA):** 48 / 19

DATE VISITED: **LODGING:**   **WHO I WENT WITH:**

WEATHER: ☀☐ ☁☐ 🌧☐ ❄☐ ⛈☐ 🌬☐   SPRING ☐ SUMMER ☐ FALL ☐ WINTER ☐

FEE(S):   **RATING:** ☆ ☆ ☆ ☆ ☆   **WILL I RETURN?** YES / NO

The park contains 26 historic and reproduction structures, mostly endangered historic buildings relocated from other locations and a few modern reconstructions. Structures include log cabins from the fur trade era, buildings from Fort Howard, and stores and public buildings from the late 19th century. The property was previously used as a prison farm with orchards managed by prisoners. Construction of a new bridge over the Fox River cut the farm off from the prison, and the land came under the jurisdiction of the State of Wisconsin Department of Natural Resources. Heritage Hill has more than 6,600 artifacts in its collection, mostly displayed within the buildings. This fantastic collection includes original artwork, books, clothing, and furnishings dating from the 17th century to the present.

STAMP

HIGH CLIFF STATE PARK

COUNTY: CALUMET   **ESTABLISHED:** 1954   **AREA (AC/HA):** 1,147 / 464

DATE VISITED: **LODGING:**   **WHO I WENT WITH:**

WEATHER: ☀☐ ☁☐ ☔☐ ❄☐ ⛆☐ 🌊☐   SPRING ☐ SUMMER ☐ FALL ☐ WINTER ☐

FEE(S):   **RATING:** ☆ ☆ ☆ ☆ ☆   **WILL I RETURN?** YES / NO

The park got its name from the cliffs of the Niagara Escarpment, a land formation east of the shore of Lake Winnebago that extends north through northeast Wisconsin, Upper Michigan, and Ontario to Niagara Falls and New York State. The magnificent 12-foot statue of Winnebago Indian Chief Red Bird, standing high on a huge granite rock, overlooks the lake and is a popular destination in the park. The park offers camping, picnicking, boating, swimming, fishing, and hunting. Hiking trails include the 6-mile limestone-surfaced Indian Mound Trail. The hiking trails in High Cliff offer hikers different levels of difficulty. All trails are looped and vary in length. The north shoreline of Lake Winnebago can be seen from a 40-foot-tall observation tower at the top of the escarpment. Various trails are available for biking, horseback riding, cross-country skiing, snowshoeing, and snowmobiling. Bicycles are allowed on all park roads. Trails open to bicyclists in the park include the Bike/Horse Trail and the Red Bird Trail. High Cliff has 8.5 miles of horse trails that run throughout the park. Horse rentals are not available in the park. The Bike/Horse Trail is open to bicyclists from approximately May 1 through November 15. Bicycles are not allowed on other trails in the park. High Cliff State Park has four developed boat launches. Windsurfing, kiteboarding, and paddleboarding enthusiasts can access the lake using undeveloped launches. A state park admission sticker is required to use these launches. There is a swimming area in High Cliff. There are no lifeguards. The bathhouse has flush toilets, showers, changing rooms, and open shelters. The park offers several camping options for visitors, including family camping, an outdoor group camp, and a cabin for people with disabilities. The family campground has 112 campsites (32 with electric hookups and 2 handicap accessible sites). There are also eight group campsites. Both the Butterfly Pond and Lake Winnebago have fishing opportunities. The pond may yield largemouth bass and panfish. Fish for walleye, white bass, and perch on the lake. Archery hunting and trapping are allowed in the open areas of the park during the Wisconsin state parks hunting and trapping time frame. High Cliff State Park has four picnic areas with tables, grills, water, and restrooms. Two picnic areas have playgrounds and swings. Some trails in the park are designed for skiing when there is snow on the ground. The trails are groomed for traditional skiing and are suitable for beginner and intermediate skiers.

STAMP

HOFFMAN HILLS STATE RECREATION AREA

COUNTY: DUNN   **ESTABLISHED:** 1980   **AREA (AC/HA):** 707 / 286

DATE VISITED: **LODGING:**   **WHO I WENT WITH:**

WEATHER: ☀☐ ⛅☐ 🌧☐ ❄☐ ⛈☐ 🌥☐   SPRING ☐ SUMMER ☐ FALL ☐ WINTER ☐

FEE(S):   **RATING:** ☆ ☆ ☆ ☆ ☆   **WILL I RETURN?**   YES / NO

There are more than nine miles of hiking trails in Hoffman Hills, including two miles of nature trails. You can hike through a 15-acre tallgrass prairie preserve or observe wildlife on a one-mile trail through a wetland that is handicap accessible. No bicycles, motorized vehicles, or horses are allowed on the trails. A 60-foot observation tower offers spectacular views of the surrounding area. There are three picnic areas in Hoffman Hills. Hoffman Hills is open for the regular nine-day gun deer season in November. The area is not open for any other hunting or trapping seasons. There are 9 miles of ski trails of varying difficulty, groomed for both skate and step skiing. Sledding, snowboarding, snowshoeing, and hiking are not allowed on the groomed ski trails.

STAMP

INTERSTATE STATE PARK

COUNTY: POLK   **ESTABLISHED:** 1900   **AREA (AC/HA):** 1,330 / 540

DATE VISITED: **LODGING:**   **WHO I WENT WITH:**

WEATHER: ☀☐ ☁☐ ⛆☐ ❄☐ ⛈☐ 🌊☐   SPRING ☐ SUMMER ☐ FALL ☐ WINTER ☐

FEE(S):   **RATING:** ☆ ☆ ☆ ☆ ☆   **WILL I RETURN?** YES / NO

Interstate is the oldest state park in the state of Wisconsin. Located along the scenic St. Croix National Scenic Riverway, the park provides scenic views of the river and a steep gorge called the Dalles of the St. Croix. The Ice Age Interpretive Center features film, photos, murals, and information about Wisconsin's glacial history. Visitors can climb the cliffs of the St. Croix Dalles River, canoe down the flat water, watch kayakers speeding down rapids or relax on a tour boat. Canoe rentals are available outside the park. There is a beach at Lake O' the Dalles with a beach house. There are no lifeguards there. Spring brings a great variety of field flowers. At least 10 different lava flows are exposed in the park, along with two distinct glacial deposits and traces of ancient streams, valleys, and faults. In the summer, you can hike the trails and explore the glacial sinkholes that make this park unique. There are over nine miles of hiking trails that offer many opportunities to view the spectacular scenery and natural attributes of the park. Guided hikes are offered during the summer months. Hiking trails vary in degree of difficulty. Interstate Park is a popular camping spot, with two campgrounds and a primitive group camp. There are several different areas in the park with picnic tables, fireplaces, grills, water, and restrooms. The Interstate has picnic shelters with reservations available for groups. The Interstate has approximately 12.5 miles of winter recreation trails for cross-country skiing, snowshoeing, and hiking. The St. Croix is a top-notch fishing river for almost every kind of game fish including walleyes, northern pike, muskies, and small-mouth bass. Hunting and trapping are allowed in the open areas of the park during the Wisconsin state parks hunting and trapping time frame.

STAMP

KETTLE MORAINE STATE FOREST

COUNTY: WASHINGTON **ESTABLISHED:** 1937 **AREA (AC/HA):** 22,000 / 8,903

DATE VISITED: **LODGING:** **WHO I WENT WITH:**

WEATHER: ☀☐ ⛅☐ 🌫☐ ❄☐ 🌧☐ 🌬☐ SPRING ☐ SUMMER ☐ FALL ☐ WINTER ☐

FEE(S): **RATING:** ☆ ☆ ☆ ☆ ☆ **WILL I RETURN?** YES / NO

Encompassing more than 22,000 acres of forested glacial hills, lakes, and prairies, the South Branch of the Kettle Moraine State Forest is interspersed with more than 100 miles of trails for mountain biking, horseback riding, hiking, and nature trails. You can also enjoy rowing, sailing, swimming, fishing, hunting, and winter sports. From the youngest beginner to the most avid pro, 30 miles of trails offer some of the best off-road biking in the Midwest. Hiking is available on the Scuppernong, Emma Carlin, John Muir, and Nordic trails, as well as the Ice Age National Scenic Trail. There are also several shorter self-guided nature trails. The Nordic and McMiller trails are open for skiing when there is enough snow. Camping, paddling, boating, swimming, fishing, and hunting are also available. There are two swimming beaches in the southern part of the Kettle Moraine National Forest: at Lake Ottawa and Lake Whitewater. There are no lifeguards there. Picnic tables, grills, and restrooms are located near the beaches. The "carry in, carry out" rule for state parks applies in these areas. The South Unit of Kettle Moraine State Forest has picnic tables and grills at many recreation areas and trails. In addition, there are shelters at several locations and an amphitheater at one location that can be reserved for group activities. Boat launches are located within the Forest at Ottawa Lake, Rice Lake, and Whitewater Lake. The Kettle Moraine State Forest - Southern Unit has several camping areas. There are four lakes within or adjacent to the southern unit of the Kettle Moraine State Forest. These lakes, ranging in size from 28 acres to 640 acres, have a total area of 860 acres. The main fish populations in these lakes are panfish and walleye. Muskellunge, largemouth and smallmouth bass, trout, and northern pike are also found here. Ottawa Lake has an accessible fishing pier and Whitewater Lake has two handicap accessible fishing stations. Most of the Southern Unit of the Kettle Moraine State Forest's 22,000 acres are open to hunting during established open seasons.

STAMP

KINNICKINNIC STATE PARK

COUNTY: PIERCE	ESTABLISHED: 1972	AREA (AC/HA): 1,239 / 501

DATE VISITED: **LODGING:** **WHO I WENT WITH:**

WEATHER: ☀□ ⛅□ 🌧□ ❄□ ⛈□ 🌫□ SPRING ☐ SUMMER ☐ FALL ☐ WINTER ☐

FEE(S): **RATING:** ☆ ☆ ☆ ☆ ☆ **WILL I RETURN?** YES / NO

The park where the Kinnickinnic River joins the St. Croix River. The mouth of the Kinnickinnic River forms a sandy delta where boaters can picnic and camp. Swimming, water skiing, sunbathing and windsurfing are very popular. The banks of the Kinnickinnic River are overgrown with Weymouth pines. There is a sandy swimming area on the St. Croix River. The area is marked with buoys. Anglers can fish the St. Croix River from either boat or shore. Although the St. Croix is known for its large walleyes, it has a wide variety of fish to catch. The Kinnickinnic River is a trout stream and has an excellent population of German brown trout. Visitors can also explore 10 miles of hiking trails. In the northern part of the park, the trails are fairly well marked with colored tape on posts at major intersections. There are maps at many of the intersections if you didn't take them from the entrance station. Off-road biking is only allowed on the Red Trail. Tables and grills are available at various locations throughout the park. The largest picnic area is located at the St. Croix viewpoint. Another popular picnic area is near the swimming area. Cross-country ski trails are available in winter. Hunting and trapping are allowed in the open areas of the park during the Wisconsin state parks hunting and trapping time frame.

STAMP

KOHLER-ANDRAE STATE PARK

COUNTY: SHEBOYGAN   **ESTABLISHED:** 1928   **AREA (AC/HA):** 988 / 400

DATE VISITED: **LODGING:**   **WHO I WENT WITH:**

WEATHER: ☀☐ ⛅☐ 🌧☐ ❄☐ ⛈☐ 🌬☐   SPRING ☐ SUMMER ☐ FALL ☐ WINTER ☐

FEE(S):   **RATING:** ☆ ☆ ☆ ☆ ☆   **WILL I RETURN?** YES / NO

Kohler-Andrae State Park encompasses two adjacent Wisconsin state parks located in the city of Wilson. The parks contain over 2 miles of beaches and dunes along the shore of Lake Michigan. Lake Michigan activities include fishing, boating, and swimming. The lake contains dozens of species of fish, including trout and salmon. You can fish in the fishing pond on Old Park Road. The pond is surrounded by an accessible path. Inland activities include hiking and biking. There are two nature trails and three hiking trails in the park. At Kohler-Andrae, there are many opportunities to hike along nature trails, dune cordons, or along the shoreline of Lake Michigan. Bicycles are allowed on all park roads. Off-road bicyclists are allowed on the Black River Trail. Horses are allowed on the Black River Trail. There is no boat launch in the park. Users of small craft or watercraft should be aware of wind conditions on Lake Michigan. Swimming is allowed in Lake Michigan. Caution should be exercised. There are no lifeguards. Kohler-Andrae State Park has a family campground, group campground, and accessible cabin for people with disabilities. Kohler-Andrae State Park has both an open and enclosed shelter and an amphitheater available for reservations. Hunting and trapping are allowed in the open areas of the park during the Wisconsin state parks hunting and trapping time frame. In the winter, cross-country skiing is available in the park. Cross-country skiing is available on a marked one-mile trail. The two-mile ski trail has flat or gentle slopes and passes through a variety of beautiful locations. The trail starts at the picnic area and runs through the wooded south campground.

STAMP

LAKE KEGONSA STATE PARK

COUNTY: DANE   **ESTABLISHED:** 1962   **AREA (AC/HA):** 343 / 139

DATE VISITED: **LODGING:**   **WHO I WENT WITH:**

WEATHER: ☀☐ ☁☐ ☔☐ ❄☐ ⛅☐ 🌬☐   SPRING ☐ SUMMER ☐ FALL ☐ WINTER ☐

FEE(S):   **RATING:** ☆ ☆ ☆ ☆ ☆   **WILL I RETURN?** YES / NO

Lake Kegonsa State Park offers a variety of recreational opportunities. The park offers swimming, fishing, water skiing, boating, and a boat landing. The lake is accessible by boat, canoe, kayak, sailboat, and other personal watercraft. Kegonsa Lake has a designated swimming beach, and there is a bathhouse nearby. There are no lifeguards on duty. No pets are allowed on the beach. Fishing opportunities are great, and hiking trails wind through oak woodlands, prairies, and wetlands. The park is known for its campground, beach, and approximately 5 miles of hiking trails. Kegonsa Lake is over 30 feet deep. It was created by a glacier during the last ice age about 12,000 years ago. Kegonsa Lake is a great place to fish year round. Local vendors offer boat rentals and live bait. A fishing license is required of all anglers. Kegonsa Lake is known for its many species of fish and fishing opportunities. Kegonsa Lake is best known for its walleye and panfish populations. Lake Kegonsa State Park has both family and group campgrounds. Campgrounds are open from May 1 through October 31. There are five picnic sites and two reservation picnic shelters in the park. There is a volleyball court and horseshoe pit near each shelter. Cross-country skiing is popular in the park. About five miles of trails, including the 1.2-mile White Oak nature trail, are groomed and tracked when weather and snow conditions permit. The trails are tracked for diagonal-stride skiers and groomed for skate skiers. Archery hunting and trapping are allowed in the open areas of the park during the Wisconsin state parks hunting and trapping time frame. Gun hunting is not allowed in the park.

STAMP

LAKE WISSOTA STATE PARK

COUNTY: CHIPPEWA **ESTABLISHED:** 1962 **AREA (AC/HA):** 1,062 / 430

DATE VISITED: **LODGING:** **WHO I WENT WITH:**

WEATHER: ☀☐ ☁☐ ☷☐ ❋☐ ☔☐ ☁☐ SPRING ☐ SUMMER ☐ FALL ☐ WINTER ☐

FEE(S): **RATING:** ☆ ☆ ☆ ☆ ☆ **WILL I RETURN?** YES / NO

The park offers campsites, hiking, biking, and horseback riding trails, picnic and playground areas, and a swimming beach on a man-made lake. Sailing, kayaking, and water skiing are popular summer activities on the lake. Lake Wissota State Park offers excellent access to the lake with a boat landing and trailer park on the south side of the park. Kayaks can be rented from the Friends of Lake Wissota State Park at the park office. The office also has a list of area businesses that rent fishing boats. Lake Wissota has several species of fish, including walleyes, muskies, bass, panfish, northern, catfish, and sturgeon. A Wisconsin fishing license is required. There is a permanent accessible fishing pier along the shore just west of the boat launch. The park grounds are covered with a mix of pine, hardwood forests, and prairie. Visitors can access the Old Abe State Trail and hike or bike 20 miles to Brunet Island State Park. Biking is a popular activity. Most of the park is flat, but more than 11 miles of park trails are open to off-road biking. Horseback riders have nine miles of trails in the park to ride on. A state trail pass is required for horseback riders 16 years of age and older. Camping for families and groups is available at Lake Wissota State Park. More than 200 species of birds make frequent stops at the lake during spring and fall migrations. Birdwatchers can obtain species checklists from the park office. There are four picnic shelters in the park, two of which can be rented. There are picnic areas along the lake near the beach and fishing pier. A large playground is located at the family campground, and the park has a soccer field and volleyball court. Hunting and trapping are allowed in the open areas of the park during the Wisconsin state parks hunting and trapping time frame. About eight miles of cross-country ski trails are groomed for both traditional stride and skate skiing. The park also has about 10 miles of trail open for snowshoeing.

STAMP

LAKESHORE STATE PARK

COUNTY: MILWAUKEE   **ESTABLISHED:** 1998   **AREA (AC/HA):** 22 / 8,9

DATE VISITED: **LODGING:**   **WHO I WENT WITH:**

WEATHER: ☀☐ ☁☐ 🌧☐ ❄☐ ⛈☐ 🌫☐   SPRING ☐ SUMMER ☐ FALL ☐ WINTER ☐

FEE(S):   **RATING:** ☆ ☆ ☆ ☆ ☆   **WILL I RETURN?** YES / NO

The park is an urban oasis with a small beach and accessible paved trails that connect to other Lake Michigan parks in Milwaukee and the Hank Aaron State Trail. The park has great views of the city and Lake Michigan, and there is a boat landing with overnight reservations. It is almost completely surrounded by water and connects to Urban Park via the beautiful Lakeshore State Park bridge. The park offers fishing, and running paths wind throughout the park. Fishing is allowed anywhere along the Lakeshore shoreline and behind the Summerfest's Marcus Amphitheater. Fishing from the pedestrian bridge is prohibited. There is an accessible fishing pier on the south lagoon, off the west trail of the island. The lagoons at Lakeshore are great for kayaking. Kayaks can be launched and landed on the beach or on the stone steps at the south end of the island. Winter hiking and snowshoeing are allowed in the park. Bird watching is popular, and you can see up close many of the northern waterfowl that use the park's lagoons. Hunting and trapping are not allowed at the property.

STAMP

LOST DAUPHIN STATE PARK

COUNTY: BROWN   ESTABLISHED: 1947   AREA (AC/HA): 19 / 7,7

DATE VISITED: LODGING: WHO I WENT WITH:

WEATHER: ☀☐ ⛅☐ 🌫☐ ❄☐ ⛈☐ 🌬☐   SPRING ☐ SUMMER ☐ FALL ☐ WINTER ☐

FEE(S):   RATING: ☆ ☆ ☆ ☆ ☆   WILL I RETURN?   YES / NO

Lost Dauphin State Park is located along the Fox River, just south of the town of De Pere. The park offers hiking trails and picnicking opportunities. It is located on land where Eleazer Williams, a claimant to Lost Dauphin, lived in the mid-19th century. The site features a scenic overlook of the Fox River with a bench, shelter, and swings. The flagstone foundation of the former house remains visible. Lost Dauphin State Park is operated locally by the Town of Lawrence.

STAMP

LOWER WISCONSIN STATE RIVERWAY

COUNTY: GRANT, BOUNDARY, DANE   **ESTABLISHED:** 1989   **AREA (AC/HA):** 45,000 / 18,211

DATE VISITED: **LODGING:**   **WHO I WENT WITH:**

WEATHER: ☀☐ ☁☐ ☂☐ ❄☐ ☔☐ 🌊☐   SPRING ☐ SUMMER ☐ FALL ☐ WINTER ☐

FEE(S):   **RATING:** ☆ ☆ ☆ ☆ ☆   **WILL I RETURN?** YES / NO

The Lower Wisconsin State Riverway offers a beautiful setting near large population centers. Riverway offers fishing, hunting, canoeing, boating, hiking, or horseback riding. You can also simply enjoy the views of the river while driving on country roads. The Riverway is abundant with birds and wildlife. Canoes are the most popular mode of transportation. Two-thirds of river trail users can be found on the stretch of the river between Prairie du Sac and Spring Green. Those looking for a more private experience will enjoy the middle section from Spring Green to Boscobel, and for users wanting solitude, the section below Boscobel is the most secluded. The Wisconsin River Valley is a scenic place consisting of stately bluffs, wooded valleys, and a sandy shoreline. Numerous islands provide opportunities for camping and outdoor recreation without the crowds. Camping along the Lower Wisconsin State Riverway is available on islands and sandbars, two state parks, and several private and municipal campgrounds. Wyalusing and Tower Hill state parks are along the river and have boat launches. There are two family campgrounds at Wyalusing and a small campground at Tower Hill. All sites can be reserved. Camping is restricted to no more than three days on state-owned islands and sandbars. People must take the trash they create with them. Hiking trails are located in Ferry Bluff and on Black Hawk Ridge. At Black Hawk Ridge, just south of the Sauk-Prairie area, visitors can hike through varied terrain and explore the historic battle site. A short but steep climb up Ferry Bluff will take visitors to a beautiful panorama of the Wisconsin River Valley - a view well worth the effort of the hike. There is an interesting interpretive exhibit at the end of the trail. Mountain bikes are not allowed on any of the trails, although bikes with fat tires are allowed in the winter. ATVs and other all-terrain vehicles are not permitted on the River Trail. There are approximately 20 miles of horseback riding trails in the riverway. Trails are located at Black Hawk Ridge and Millville. There are some beautiful vistas along the trails as they cross the ridges above the river valley.

STAMP

MACKENZIE CENTER

COUNTY: COLUMBIA   **ESTABLISHED:** 1930   **AREA (AC/HA):** 280 / 113,3

DATE VISITED:	**LODGING:**	**WHO I WENT WITH:**

WEATHER: ☀☐ ⛅☐ ☁☐ ❄☐ 🌧☐ 🌫☐   SPRING ☐ SUMMER ☐ FALL ☐ WINTER ☐

FEE(S):   **RATING:** ☆ ☆ ☆ ☆ ☆   **WILL I RETURN?** YES / NO

The MacKenzie Center has interpretive trails, exhibits, museums, and programming available for school and youth groups. The MacKenzie Center is a wonderful place to visit and learn about the natural world. The logging museum is located in a log home that was built in the early 1880s near Grantsburg. Inside are images of Wisconsin's logging industry in the late 19th century, historic tools used for timber harvests, and two dioramas depicting logging practices. The sawmill exhibit near the logging museum provides an opportunity to see how lumber was processed in the early days of Wisconsin's booming lumber industry. Visitors can also learn how sugar and maple syrup are made. MacKenzie is home to a number of self-guided nature trails. The nature trail begins at the entrance to the wildlife area, winds through the woods, and connects to the logging museum. The trail system at the south end of the property is approximately 0.5 mile from the main parking area. The southern trail system includes five nature trails, one of which is wheelchair accessible. The MacKenzie Center is not open to hunting during public hunting seasons, but the MacKenzie Center hosts several Learn to Hunt events throughout the year. The MacKenzie Center has a grassy picnic area with a shelter by reservation for visitors. The shelter is located on a lawn adjacent to a wooded area. The shelter has ample parking, picnic tables, and grills. A flush toilet is located nearby. The shelter can be reserved.

STAMP

MENOMINEE RIVER STATE RECREATION AREA

COUNTY: MARINETTE   **ESTABLISHED:** 2010   **AREA (AC/HA):** 7,652 / 3,096

DATE VISITED: **LODGING:**   **WHO I WENT WITH:**

WEATHER: ☀☐ ⛅☐ ☔☐ ❄☐ ⛅☐ 🌫☐   SPRING ☐ SUMMER ☐ FALL ☐ WINTER ☐

FEE(S):   **RATING:** ☆ ☆ ☆ ☆ ☆   **WILL I RETURN?** YES / NO

The area extends for several miles along the banks of the scenic Menominee River in northeastern Wisconsin. It is possible to canoe the river among tall pines, rock outcrops, and waterfalls or enjoy other areas of this quiet property for primitive camping, hiking, fishing, and hunting. This beautiful wildlife viewing area with campsites and boat access points along the river caters to wildlife watchers. The property includes a rustic canoe landing at Quiver Falls, a concrete boat landing at Saler Landing on Rattie Road, and a gravel boat landing in Pemene on Horseshoe Road. Other marinas are located off the farm and on the Michigan side of the river. Most of the river is wide and gentle, with a few rapids. Pemene Falls to the south is a mandatory portage (Michigan side). Fishing is available in the Menominee River. The Menominee River is known for its smallmouth bass fishing. Many other fish species are present as well. Hiking opportunities are available on the Pemene Falls Trail, which is located in the Pemene Falls unit. The Sand Portage hiking trail is located in the Piers Gorge unit on the property. Other trails and logging roads exist on the property but are not maintained and managed as designated trails. Hunting and trapping is allowed on the property during legal hunting and trapping seasons. The property is open for snowshoeing and ungroomed cross-country skiing. Marinette County ATV/snowmobile trails cross parts of the property.

STAMP

MERRICK STATE PARK

COUNTY: BUFFALO   **ESTABLISHED:** 1932   **AREA (AC/HA):** 320 / 130

DATE VISITED: **LODGING:**   **WHO I WENT WITH:**

WEATHER: ☀☐ ⛅☐ ☔☐ ❄☐ ⛈☐ 🌊☐   SPRING ☐ SUMMER ☐ FALL ☐ WINTER ☐

FEE(S):   **RATING:** ☆ ☆ ☆ ☆ ☆   **WILL I RETURN?** YES / NO

The park is located on the beautiful floodplains of the Mississippi River. Merrick State Park offers many recreational opportunities that can be enjoyed year-round. All campgrounds on the island and some campsites to the south have access to the river for mooring watercraft or fishing directly from these sites. There are 65 individual campsites in three campgrounds and a 50-person group tents-only campsite at Merrick State Park. Registered campers may moor boats overnight at each campground. There are 2 miles of hiking trails and two boat landing sites provide easy boat launches. Picnic areas are located along the Mississippi River, offering tables, access to fishing spots, wildlife viewing, and the opportunity to simply relax. Hiking trails run through the park for two miles, connecting most areas. Visitors can enjoy a variety of experiences, including prairies, wetlands, and the flood plain of hardwood forests in the lower elevations of the park. The trails offer relatively easy hiking experiences suitable for most age groups. Picnic sites are located along the Mississippi River offering tables, water, access to fishing opportunities, wildlife viewing, and opportunities to relax. One of the picnic areas near the lower boat launch is open to pets on a leash. The park playground is located halfway between the north and south campgrounds, next to the parking lot at the nature center shelter. The Mississippi River is alive with large and smallmouth bass, bluegills, crappies, and other species. Merrick State Park offers two boat launches that can accommodate most motorized boats. There is ample parking at both marinas. A canoe landing adjacent to the lower marina provides easy access for kayakers. The quiet backwaters adjacent to the river provide a great opportunity for those looking for a quiet, sporty experience on the water. Enjoy the sun, wildlife, and wilderness in the river, which is five minutes from the marina. The self-guided canoe trail begins and ends near the lower boat landing. Be sure to follow the canoe trail signs. Some sections of the trail wind through shallow water. In some places, kayaks and boats go together. Kayak rentals are available daily from Memorial Day through Labor Day. Cross-country skiing is a favorite winter activity in Merrick. The natural snow surface of the trail system and undeveloped areas in the park are available for skiers who like to spend time off-trail. Hunting and trapping are allowed in the open areas of the park while Wisconsin State Parks hunting and trapping regulations are in effect. --

----

STAMP

MILL BLUFF STATE PARK

COUNTY: MONROE, JUNEAU   **ESTABLISHED:** 1936   **AREA (AC/HA):** 1,337 / 541

DATE VISITED:	**LODGING:**	**WHO I WENT WITH:**

WEATHER: ☀☐ ☁☐ 🌧☐ ❄☐ ⛈☐ 🌫☐   SPRING ☐ SUMMER ☐ FALL ☐ WINTER ☐

FEE(S):   **RATING:** ☆ ☆ ☆ ☆ ☆   **WILL I RETURN?** YES / NO

Part of the Ice Age National Scientific Reserve, Mill Bluff State Park offers spectacular views of scenic rock formations. The park protects several prominent sandstone bluffs 80 feet to 200 feet high that formed as sea stacks 12,000 years ago in Glacial Lake Wisconsin. As a result, these bluffs are steep and angular, dissimilar to the rounded terrain more typical of the eastern half of the United States. Campsites, picnic areas, a shelter, hiking trails, and a swimming pond are located in this park just outside of Camp Douglas. Mill Bluff State Park has a rustic family campground with 21 sites. The campground is open from late May through September. There are two picnic sites in Mill Bluff, east and west of Funnel Road. Each has a shelter, picnic tables, grills, water, restrooms, and parking. A 2.5 acre pond with clean, cool water from underground springs and 250 feet of white sand beach is available for public swimming. There are no bike trails at the park, but Juneau County's 15-mile-long Omaha Bike Trail can be reached from the park via County Highway W to County Highway C into Camp Douglas. The Omaha bike trail also connects to the Elroy-Sparta State Trail and the 400 State Trail in Elroy. There are more than two miles of hiking trails at Mill Bluff offering views of the park's mesas, buttes, and pinnacles. Stairs lead to the top of Mill Bluff. Pets are not permitted on the nature trail or in the picnic and swimming areas. Although Mill Bluff State Park is not staffed during the winter, the park is still open. Visitors often hike, snowshoe or cross-country ski using marked trails. Trails are not groomed or maintained for winter use. Hunting and trapping is allowed in open areas of the park while Wisconsin State Parks hunting and trapping regulations are in effect. The park allows small game and deer hunting.

STAMP

MIRROR LAKE STATE PARK

COUNTY: SAUK   **ESTABLISHED:** 1962   **AREA (AC/HA):** 2,192 / 882

DATE VISITED: **LODGING:**   **WHO I WENT WITH:**

WEATHER: ☀☐ ☁☐ 🌧☐ ❄☐ ⛅☐ 🌫☐   SPRING ☐ SUMMER ☐ FALL ☐ WINTER ☐

FEE(S):   **RATING:** ☆ ☆ ☆ ☆ ☆   **WILL I RETURN?** YES / NO

Mirror Lake State Park offers recreational opportunities for everyone. Boat, canoe, and kayak rentals are available in summer from the park concession stand. There are approximately 9 miles of trails for off-road cycling enthusiasts that are open from May 1 through October 31 each year, depending on weather and conditions. These trails are not open to bicycles, including fat tire bikes, between November 1 and April 30 due to cross-country skiing and trail and turf maintenance. These trails include the Hastings, Fern Dell, Turtleville, and Wild Rice Trails and are located on the south side of Fern Dell Road. The 400 State Trail is a 15-minute drive from Mirror Lake State Park in Reedsburg. There are two boat landings on Mirror Lake. One is located within the state park and hosts concessions and boat rentals. The other is the town of Delton launch which is located on Lakeview Road off State Highway 23 at the west end of the lake. Mirror Lake has a swimming beach with restrooms nearby. There are no lifeguards. No pets are allowed on the beach. Mirror Lake is slow-no-wake for the entire lake. Mirror Lake State Park has 151 family camping sites in three separate campgrounds and seven group sites. The campsites are mostly wooded, with beautiful pine and oak trees making up most of the forest. Each site has a fire pit and picnic table, and most have a sandy camping area. Both Mirror Lake and Dell Creek offer fishing opportunities. Dell Creek is 10.5 miles long and flows into Mirror Lake. It has cool water and suitable hiding places for trout, but because there is no spawning gravel, the fishery is dependent on stocking. There are more than 19 miles of hiking trails in Mirror Lake State Park. There are three separate picnic sites at Mirror Lake State Park. There is an accessible picnic shelter at each site. Both shelters - Beach and Bluewater Bay - can be reserved. This large picnic area surrounding the swimming beach at Mirror Lake State Park is equipped with picnic tables and grills. Mirror Lake State Park offers numerous winter recreation opportunities, including groomed trails for cross-country skiing, snowshoeing and hiking trails, winter camping, and ice fishing. Hunting and trapping are allowed in the open areas of the park while Wisconsin State Parks hunting and trapping regulations are in effect.

STAMP

NATURAL BRIDGE STATE PARK

COUNTY: SAUK **ESTABLISHED:** 1972 **AREA (AC/HA):** 530 / 210

DATE VISITED: **LODGING:** **WHO I WENT WITH:**

WEATHER: ☀□ ☁□ 🌧□ ❄□ ⛈□ 🌬□ SPRING ☐ SUMMER ☐ FALL ☐ WINTER ☐

FEE(S): **RATING:** ☆ ☆ ☆ ☆ ☆ **WILL I RETURN?** YES / NO

Natural Bridge State Park provides a variety of outdoor recreation opportunities to visitors year-round. The park is for day use only. Natural Bridge State Park has a natural sandstone arch created by the eroding effects of wind and water. The bridge opening is 25 feet high by 35 feet wide. This weathered formation was missed by the glaciers during the last Ice Age. Near the bridge is a rock shelter used by native people when the glacier was melting 11,000 years ago. The hills of the park are covered with oaks and other hardwoods. On some of the ridge tops there are small prairie remnants with grasses and cacti. There are approximately 4 miles of hiking trails at Natural Bridge. All trails begin at the large parking area on County Highway C. A nature trail with information on Native American plant use runs through part of the state park's natural area. South of the highway is a 2-mile hiking trail through the woods. Climbing the arch itself or entering the shelter is prohibited due to the protection of the natural area. The park's natural land cover is primarily oak woodland, with open fields and stretches of native prairie. Many wildflowers bloom here throughout the growing season, and birdwatchers may see species such as vultures, woodpeckers, and bald eagles in winter. There is a large picnic area with tables next to the County Highway C parking lot. Cross-country skiing is allowed in the park, but there are no groomed ski trails. Winter hiking and snowshoeing are allowed throughout the park. Hunting and trapping are allowed in the open areas of the park while Wisconsin State Parks hunting and trapping regulations are in effect.

STAMP

NELSON DEWEY STATE PARK

COUNTY: GRANT   **ESTABLISHED:** 1935   **AREA (AC/HA):** 756 / 306

DATE VISITED: **LODGING:**   **WHO I WENT WITH:**

WEATHER: ☼☐ ☁☐ ☂☐ ❄☐ ⛅☐ ☁☐   SPRING ☐ SUMMER ☐ FALL ☐ WINTER ☐

FEE(S):   **RATING:** ☆ ☆ ☆ ☆ ☆   **WILL I RETURN?**   YES / NO

Nelson Dewey State Park overlooks the Mississippi River from a 500-foot bluff. The land was once part of the Stonefield estate of Nelson Dewey, the state's first governor. Nelson Dewey State Park offers over two miles of hiking trails. Trails can vary in difficulty. Five of the trails in Nelson Dewey State Park are less than a mile long but offer a variety of scenery. Several trails in the park offer great views of the Mississippi River Valley. The park is home to the Dewey House and the nearby Stonefield Historic Site. Guests can enjoy a wealth of outdoor activities, from exciting programs at the park to bird watching and wildlife viewing at Dewey Heights Prairie. Nelson Dewey State Park offers camping for individuals, families, and small and large groups. Grocery and camping supplies and laundry facilities are available in Cassville, about 2 miles south of the park. Nelson Dewey State Park does not have river access. A boat landing is in the city of Cassville at Riverside Park. There is no fishing available at Nelson Dewey State Park. A popular fishing spot is Riverside Park in Cassville. There are three picnic areas within the park; Mound Point, Dewey Heights, and Cedar Point. Picnic tables and grills are available at all three areas. The Dewey Heights picnic area has two handicap accessible picnic shelters and handicap accessible restrooms. During the winter months, visitors can hike, ski, or snowshoe on the trails. Hunting and trapping are allowed in the open areas of the park while Wisconsin State Parks hunting and trapping regulations are in effect.

STAMP

NEW GLARUS WOODS STATE PARK

COUNTY: GREEN	ESTABLISHED: 1934	AREA (AC/HA): 435 / 175

DATE VISITED: **LODGING:**   **WHO I WENT WITH:**

WEATHER: ☀□ ☁□ 🌦□ 🌧□ 🌩□ 🌬□   SPRING ☐ SUMMER ☐ FALL ☐ WINTER ☐

FEE(S):   **RATING:** ☆ ☆ ☆ ☆ ☆   **WILL I RETURN?** YES / NO

The park encompasses rolling hills covered in a mix of forest and prairie. The Sugar River State Trail connects to the park, making the park accessible by bike. This trail also connects to the Badger State Trail. The park offers camping and picnicking. In the summer, visitors can enjoy more than 24 miles of trails for hiking and exploring, or bring a rod and fishing kit to fish in the many streams that flow through the park. Hiking trails in New Glarus Woods wind among mature forests and restored prairies. Visitors can enjoy hiking up and down the undulating terrain while observing wildlife such as deer, squirrels, turkeys, various species of songbirds, and woodpeckers. Bicycles are allowed on all paved surfaces within the park and campgrounds. New Glarus Woods offers family and group campsites. New Glarus Woods has small, primitive campgrounds that provide 18 drive-in campsites for tent, pop-up, and small (RV) recreational vehicle camping as well as 14 "walk-to" sites for tent camping. New Glarus Woods provides one large picnic area with cooking grills and picnic tables. In the picnic area, there is a large playground, open-air picnic shelter with lights and electricity, vault toilet restrooms, and drinking fountains. A small picnic area with grills and tables is next to the walk-to campsites. Bicycles are not allowed on hiking trails. The Sugar River Trail Spur passes through the campground and connects to the 24-mile Sugar River State Trail. Bike rentals are available in the village of New Glarus at the Sugar River State Trailhead. In the winter, visitors can enjoy cross-country skiing and snowshoeing. Hunting and trapping are allowed in the open areas of the park while Wisconsin State Parks hunting and trapping regulations are in effect.

STAMP

NEWPORT STATE PARK

COUNTY: DOOR **ESTABLISHED:** 1964 **AREA (AC/HA):** 2,373 / 960

DATE VISITED: **LODGING:** **WHO I WENT WITH:**

WEATHER: ☀☐ ⛅☐ 🌧☐ ⛈☐ ☁☐ 🌬☐ SPRING ☐ SUMMER ☐ FALL ☐ WINTER ☐

FEE(S): **RATING:** ☆ ☆ ☆ ☆ ☆ **WILL I RETURN?** YES / NO

This park is located near Lake Michigan shoreline and offers more than 30 trails for hiking. The park offers hiking, swimming, fishing, backpacking, skiing, and snowshoeing. There are evergreen and deciduous forests, wetlands, and upland meadows. The park has an interpretive center and nature program. Newport State Park is one of the darkest areas in the state, making it one of the best places to observe the night sky. It is the prime destination for those who are interested in astronomy or stargazing. Located at the far end of the Door Peninsula and on the shores of Lake Michigan, Newport State Park is one of the darkest places in the state. The park is the place to experience what a dark sky really looks like, making it the perfect place for everyone from casual stargazers to astronomers. Newport has been recognized as a Dark Sky Park by the International Dark-Sky Association, one of 18 in the United States and only the second in the Midwest. Bike trails consist mostly of hard pack dirt. Trails are considered easy to moderate, with no great elevation changes. Hiking is also allowed on all bike trails. About 17 miles of trail are open to off-road bicycles. There is no boat launch in the park. Users of small craft or watercraft should be aware of wind conditions on Lake Michigan. Newport State Park offers rustic backpack camping for visitors. Camping is only allowed in designated campgrounds. There is a picnic area on Newport Bay by parking lot #3. You can reserve an available shelter in the picnic area at Newport State Park. Fishing is available in Lake Michigan and Lake Europe in the northern part of the park. Over 26 miles of trails are open for cross-country skiing. There are 12 miles of groomed trails for Nordic skiing and 2 miles for skate skiing. About 5 miles of trails are open for snowshoeing. Hunting and trapping is allowed in open areas of the park while Wisconsin State Parks hunting and trapping regulations are in effect.

STAMP

NORTHERN HIGHLAND AMERICAN LEGION STATE FOREST

COUNTY: VILAS, ONEIDA, IRON   **ESTABLISHED:** 1925   **AREA (AC/HA):** 236,000 / 95,506

DATE VISITED: **LODGING:**   **WHO I WENT WITH:**

WEATHER: ☀☐ ☁☐ 🌧☐ ❄☐ ⛅☐ 🌊☐   SPRING☐ SUMMER☐ FALL☐ WINTER☐

FEE(S):   **RATING:** ☆ ☆ ☆ ☆ ☆   **WILL I RETURN?** YES / NO

The forest offers a wide variety of outdoor recreational activities including camping, hiking, biking, snowmobiling, boating, fishing, hunting, and bird watching. In addition to recreational activities, research programs are also conducted. Lakes, streams, and rivers provide hundreds of miles of water to explore by canoe or kayak, and many allow motorized boats. The forest is home to 224 species of birds, nearly three-quarters of the species found in the state of Wisconsin. All-Terrain Vehicles are not allowed anywhere on the Northern Highland American Legion State Forest. Except for the nature trails, Fallison, Trout Lake, Star Lake, and Raven's yellow loop, biking is allowed on all roads and trails. Designated mountain bike trails require a state trail pass, which can be purchased by self-registering at the trail heads. Trails designated for biking are McNaughton, Madeline, Lumberjack, and Raven. There are two trails on or near the forest that have suitable surfaces for all bikes. The Bearskin State Trail has trail heads in Minocqua and on Highway K near Highway 51. Also, the surrounding area towns maintain a paved bike trail that runs from the Boulder Junction, through Crystal, Firefly, Muskie, North Trout, and South Trout campgrounds, and on to St. Germain. The forest provides a variety of modern, rustic, group, and primitive camping opportunities. Some campgrounds offer accessible facilities. Seven hiking trails and four nature trails have been established in NHAL. There are also hundreds of miles of old logging roads, less traveled town roads, logging roads, and snowmobile trails that offer good hiking opportunities. There are no designated riding trails on the state forest. However, there are many places where horses may be ridden within the property, such as public roads, old logging roads, and snowmobile trails when not covered with snow. Horses are not allowed on campgrounds, beaches, designated hiking trails, or nature trails. The NHAL is home to the largest concentration of lakes in Wisconsin. With over 900 lakes and over 300 miles of rivers and streams, water recreation is often one of the main reasons people visit NHAL. There are many picnic areas in the NHAL. NHAL has four beautiful and scenic cross-country ski trails: Escanaba, Madeline, McNaughton, and Raven. State passes are required on these trails. Because they are cross-country trails, snowshoeing, hiking, and pets are not allowed on these trails in the winter. Hunting is permitted in the forest.

STAMP

PATTISON STATE PARK

COUNTY: DOUGLAS   **ESTABLISHED:** 1920   **AREA (AC/HA):** 1,400 / 566

DATE VISITED: **LODGING:**   **WHO I WENT WITH:**

WEATHER: ☀☐ ⛅☐ 🌧☐ ⛈☐ ☁☐ 🌬☐   SPRING ☐ SUMMER ☐ FALL ☐ WINTER ☐

FEE(S):   **RATING:** ☆ ☆ ☆ ☆ ☆   **WILL I RETURN?** YES / NO

Located on the Black River, Pattison State Park includes two waterfalls: one is the tallest waterfall in Wisconsin, 165-foot Big Manitou Falls, and the other is the smallest waterfall in Wisconsin, 31-foot Little Manitou Falls. There are plenty of activities to enjoy on the Black River, from swimming to fishing and boating to paddleboarding. Recreational fishing opportunities in the park are limited. There is no sport fish population in the lake. There is occasional fishing in the Black River below Big Manitou Falls, although numbers have declined since the DNR stopped stocking this area. For up-to-date information on seasons, size limits, and numbers of fish, contact the park office. This park features a lake with a beach, a nature center, a campground, and scenic hiking trails. Pattison State Park has over 7 miles of trails. The Black River begins its winding journey about 22 miles southwest of the park at Black Lake on the Wisconsin-Minnesota border. As it passes through Pattison State Park, it drops 31 feet over Little Manitou Falls, forms Interfalls Lake, and then reaches the spectacular Big Manitou Falls. Hike the trails along the Black River for spectacular views of the falls. Pattison State Park has one campground with 59 family camping sites, as well as three backpacking sites. There are three picnic areas in Pattison with tables, grills, water, and restrooms. The largest of these is located near the beach. There are playground equipment near the main picnic area. Pattison State Park has an enclosed building with a shelter at the main picnic area that can be rented. Pattison's 300-foot sandy beach at Interfalls Lake offers excellent sunbathing, a beautiful bathhouse, and an adjacent picnic area. The beach is unguarded. Swimming beyond the lifeline, in the river, or by the waterfalls is dangerous. The park is also a nice place for geology enthusiasts, with dark magma rocks throughout the park. You can even see a trail of earthquake and lava damage that hit the area billions of years ago. Almost 200 species of birds, 54 species of mammals, and many reptiles and amphibians can be observed in the park. There are 5.5 miles of classic cross-country ski trails in the park. The difficulty of the trails ranges from beginner to moderate. Three interconnected loops begin at the campground. Pattison State Park has many informal trails for snowshoeing in the winter. Hunting and trapping are allowed in the open areas of the park while Wisconsin State Parks hunting and trapping regulations are in effect.

STAMP

PENINSULA STATE PARK

COUNTY: DOOR   **ESTABLISHED:** 1909   **AREA (AC/HA):** 3,776 / 1,528

DATE VISITED: **LODGING:**   **WHO I WENT WITH:**

WEATHER: ☀☐ ⛅☐ 🌧☐ ❄☐ ⛈☐ 🌬☐   SPRING ☐ SUMMER ☐ FALL ☐ WINTER ☐

FEE(S):   **RATING:** ☆ ☆ ☆ ☆ ☆   **WILL I RETURN?** YES / NO

The park is known for its bluffs, which reach 150 feet into the air, allowing for some impressive views from the top. Many people consider Peninsula to be the most complete park in Wisconsin. When you see its abundant offerings, it's easy to see why. Starting near the Fish Creek entrance to the Park, the fine gravel on the relatively flat Sunset Trail accommodates bicycles, wheelchairs, and hikers. The trail traverses Weborg Marsh, cedar and maple trees, and cliff communities. The Sunset Bike Route connects to a return route at Nicolet Beach, for four additional miles on the Park's scenic back roads. Hidden Bluff is a scenic 0.75-mile spur of the Sunset Trail, providing access to the nature center and a shortcut for bicyclists traveling to and from Nicolet Bay. Nicolet Beach offers a swimming area (no lifeguard), kayak and other watercraft rentals, a snack bar, and plenty of sand for sunbathing. Exploring the peninsula from the water provides amazing views, excellent fishing, and great fun. The park's eight-mile shoreline is popular with power boaters, sailors, and kayakers. There is a launch ramp located in Nicolet Bay. There is day use only parking for vehicles and trailers near the ramp. Campers on the peninsula have the option to overnight a trailer in the parking lot at the amphitheater. Kayaks are often launched in Tennison Bay, which has a shallow draft. Overnight anchoring is allowed off Horseshoe Island and in Nicolet Bay, outside of the designated boating and launching area. Weborg pier is a hotspot for hooking smallmouth and rock bass or perhaps brown trout. Peninsula is Wisconsin's most popular camping destination. Peninsula State Park's five campgrounds have a total of 468 family sites, as well as three group sites for tent camping. Tennison Bay campground has campsites available for winter camping. Peninsula has an 18-hole golf course and a six-hole learning Short Course. Peninsula has a total of 20 miles of hiking trails. Peninsula has several picnic areas; Fish Creek (near park headquarters), Nelson Point, Nicolet Beach, and Pines Area, Eagle Terrace, Weborg Point, and Welcker's Point. These areas have tables, charcoal grills, and toilets. The Peninsula has 16 miles of groomed, mostly double-tracked ski trails. Skaters have access to six miles of trails groomed for both classical and skate skiing. Peninsula offers six miles of designated snowshoe and hiking trails in the winter. Bow hunting and trapping is allowed in open areas of the park during the hunting and trapping season in Wisconsin state parks.

STAMP

PERROT STATE PARK

COUNTY: TREMPEALEAU   **ESTABLISHED:** 1918   **AREA (AC/HA):** 1,200 / 485

DATE VISITED: **LODGING:**   **WHO I WENT WITH:**

WEATHER: ☼☐ ☁☐ ☂☐ ❄☐ ☔☐ ☁☐   SPRING ☐ SUMMER ☐ FALL ☐ WINTER ☐

FEE(S):   **RATING:** ☆ ☆ ☆ ☆ ☆   **WILL I RETURN?** YES / NO

Perrot State Park's 1,200 acres are nestled among 500-foot bluffs where the Trempealeau and Mississippi rivers meet. Enjoy breathtaking river views from the hiking trails in this park, known for its natural, archaeological, and historical resources. There is direct access for bicyclists from the campground to the 24-mile Great River State Trail. There is also a marked canoe trail in Trempealeau Bay. Canoes can be rented at the park in season. Perrot State Park offers several family campsites and four walk-in group campsites. There is direct bicycle access from the campground to the Great River State Trail. There is a boat landing on the Trempealeau River that provides access to Trempealeau Bay and the Mississippi River via a railroad bridge. There is fishing available on the shore. Please note that the Trempealeau River is shallow as it flows through the park and the water level changes throughout the year. Fishing in Trempealeau Bay varies depending on the time of year and changing water levels. There are other areas nearby that provide shore fishing and boat access. There is a boat landing in Trempealeau with access to the Mississippi River. Trempealeau Lakes Recreation Area offers fishing from shore, an accessible fishing pier, and boat docks. There are 12.5 miles of hiking trails in the park. Many of them lead to the top of the bluffs and provide a unique opportunity to enjoy scenic views of the Mississippi River Valley. The trails on the bluffs are steep and some have steps or stairs. For a closer view of the river and Trempealeau Bay, hike the Riverview Trail, which runs the entire length of the park. Perrot State Park has six picnic areas along the trails and around the nature center. Here you can relax after hiking the bluffs, watch wildlife, or sit below the nature center and watch a beautiful sunset over Trempealeau Bay. Each picnic area has grills, and bathrooms and water are available in season. There is a picnic shelter near the nature center with no reservations available. A volleyball net and horseshoe pits are near the nature center. Horseshoes and volleyballs are available for checkout at the park headquarters. When snow conditions permit, nine miles of trail are groomed and tracked for cross-country skiing. Skate skiing is allowed only on a one-mile section of trail in the campground. Hiking, snowshoeing, and pets are not allowed on groomed ski trails. Hunting and trapping is allowed in open areas of the park while Wisconsin State Parks hunting and trapping regulations are in effect.

STAMP

POINT BEACH STATE FOREST

COUNTY: MANITOWOC   **ESTABLISHED:** 1938   **AREA (AC/HA):** 3,029 / 1,225

DATE VISITED: **LODGING:**   **WHO I WENT WITH:**

WEATHER: ☀□ ⛅□ 🌧□ ❄□ 🌦□ 🌊□   SPRING ☐ SUMMER ☐ FALL ☐ WINTER ☐

FEE(S):   **RATING:** ☆ ☆ ☆ ☆ ☆   **WILL I RETURN?** YES / NO

The forest offers a variety of outdoor adventures such as hiking, biking, swimming, picnicking, fishing, and boating. There are 17 miles of hiking trails through the forest, the longest of which is over 7 miles long. There are two shelters at Point Beach. There are picnic areas near the shelter, as well as picnic areas where you can sit and enjoy Lake Michigan. There is also a playground, volleyball courts, and a baseball field. The picnic areas at Point Beach State Forest are fully developed with picnic tables, outdoor grills, clean drinking water, and restrooms. Point Beach State Forest offers 127 camping sites, many of which are equipped with electrical hookups, making for excellent camping. There are 6 miles of sandy beach along Lake Michigan for swimming in the woods. There are no lifeguards. No campfires are allowed on the beach. A separate beach is set aside for dogs. There is no boat launching area on the forest. Persons using small watercraft or boating equipment should be aware of wind conditions on Lake Michigan. A popular site in the area is Rawley Point Lighthouse, which has been operated and maintained by the U.S. Coast Guard since 1853. For cyclists, there are well-laid bike paths such as the Ridges Trail. The Ridges Trail has three connecting loops for off-road biking. The Rawley Point Bicycle Trail starts at the lodge parking lot and goes south through pine and hemlock forest for 5 miles. The trail consists of a hard-packed limestone base. It connects to the Mariners Trail [exit DNR], a 7-mile paved trail along the Lake Michigan shoreline to Two Rivers and Manitowoc. The Red Pine Trail begins at the parking lot west of County Highway O across from the forest entrance road. The trail is 3.1 miles long. This trail is open to mountain bikes and hikers in the summer and skiers in the winter. The forest also offers a variety of winter activities with well-marked ski trails and snowmobiling. Hunting and trapping is allowed on the property during legal hunting and trapping seasons.

STAMP

POTAWATOMI STATE PARK

COUNTY: DOOR   **ESTABLISHED:** 1928   **AREA (AC/HA):** 1,200 / 485

DATE VISITED: **LODGING:**   **WHO I WENT WITH:**

WEATHER: ☀□ ⛅□ 🌫□ ❄□ ☁□ 🌬□   SPRING □ SUMMER □ FALL □ WINTER □

FEE(S):   **RATING:** ☆ ☆ ☆ ☆ ☆   **WILL I RETURN?** YES / NO

The park is named after a tribe that inhabited the shores and islands of Green Bay when Europeans first settled the area. The tribe was called the Bo-De-Wad-Me, which means "keeper of the fire". The park has several hiking trails and is the eastern terminus of the Ice Age National Scenic Trail. Park trails are used for hiking, biking, cross-country skiing, and snowmobiling. The park has four groomed cross-country ski trails totaling about 8.5 miles. Approximately eight miles of off-road bike paths run through the park. Bicycle parking is available in Parking Lot 1 near the picnic areas along the shoreline. Hikers can also ride bicycles on all park roads. Potawatomi State Park has several picnic areas along the shoreline of Sturgeon Bay, as well as a viewpoint overlooking the park's old ski hill. There are playgrounds in the picnic area at parking lot 2 and at Daisy Field campground. A shelter can be reserved at the picnic area along the south shore. The shelter has a fireplace and electrical outlets. Potawatomi State Park has family and group campsites and an accessible cabin for people with disabilities. Potawatomi State Park is the base for boating, kayaking, canoeing, fishing, SCUBA diving, and water skiing on Green Bay. Over two miles of shoreline provide many scenic views and recreational opportunities. The park has a boat landing in Sawyer Harbor, a sheltered cove at the mouth of Sturgeon Bay. Canoe, kayak, and paddleboat rentals are available in the park. There is a fish cleaning station at the boat launch. Anglers 16 years or older must have a valid Wisconsin fishing license. Anglers of any age may check out basic fishing equipment free of charge at the park office. The accessible fishing pier is located in the picnic area, on the park's south shoreline. Due to the rocky shoreline, there is no beach for swimming in Potawatomi Park. The terrain is gently rolling and upland, surrounded by steep slopes and rugged limestone cliffs. Hunting and trapping are allowed in the open areas of the park while Wisconsin State Parks hunting and trapping regulations are in effect.

STAMP

RIB MOUNTAIN STATE PARK

COUNTY: MARATHON   **ESTABLISHED:** 1927   **AREA (AC/HA):** 1,528 / 618

DATE VISITED: **LODGING:**   **WHO I WENT WITH:**

WEATHER: ☀☐ ⛅☐ ☁☐ ❄☐ 🌧☐ 🌬☐   SPRING ☐ SUMMER ☐ FALL ☐ WINTER ☐

FEE(S):   **RATING:** ☆ ☆ ☆ ☆ ☆   **WILL I RETURN?** YES / NO

This billion-year-old hill is one of the oldest geological formations on Earth. The park is an excellent day use facility, offering picnic areas, hiking trails, a scenic amphitheater, an indoor meeting place, and picnic shelters. The park's top offers spectacular views of the Wausau area and the Wisconsin River. Granite Peak Ski Resort is located on the north face of the mountain and offers downhill skiing and snowboarding. There are more than 13 miles of hiking trails at Rib Mountain, with over eight miles accessible to people with disabilities. Pets are permitted in the park on the trails when on an 8-foot leash. There are no groomed cross-country ski trails in the park. Winter hiking and snowshoeing are allowed in most areas of the park. A 2-mile groomed snowshoe trail on the Middle Yellow Trail loop is popular. Users can access this trail from the parking lot south of the entrance station. Picnicking is very popular at Rib Mountain. There are several picnic areas with tables, two playgrounds, shelters with reservations, and an amphitheater with reservations at the top of the park. Pets are not allowed in the picnic areas. Hunting and trapping are allowed in the open areas of the park while Wisconsin State Parks hunting and trapping regulations are in effect.

STAMP

RICHARD BONG STATE RECREATION AREA

COUNTY: KENOSHA   **ESTABLISHED:** 1963   **AREA (AC/HA):** 4,515 / 1,827

DATE VISITED: **LODGING:**   **WHO I WENT WITH:**

WEATHER: ☀☐ ⛅☐ 🌫☐ ❄☐ 🌧☐ 🌬☐   SPRING ☐ SUMMER ☐ FALL ☐ WINTER ☐

FEE(S):   **RATING:** ☆ ☆ ☆ ☆ ☆   **WILL I RETURN?** YES / NO

Once designated to be a jet fighter base, Richard Bong State Recreation Area is named after Major Richard I. Bong, a Poplar, WI native who was America's leading air ace during World War II. The area has a network of 16 miles of hiking trails that allow you to explore all the wildlife in the area. There is swimming, boating, kayaking, and fishing available. There is a 200-foot beach. The recreation area has a boat launch (electric motors only). Shore fishing is available on Wolf Lake and at the city fish pond. Wisconsin fishing licenses are required. There are two family (modern) campgrounds with a total of 217 campsites, 54 with electric hookups. Six group campsites can accommodate 225 campers. There is also a cabin designed specifically for people with disabilities. The park is also a great choice for those looking for a winter camping vacation. The park's trail network transforms into a beautiful cross-country ski trail. There is also great sledding for kids. This prairie contains 8.3 miles of mountain bike trails. Off-road bike trails are available north of Highway 142. Other recreational activities include high power rocketry, dogsledding, falconry, ATV sports, land sailing, horseback riding, hunting, and ultralight aviation. There are nearly 6.5 miles of ATV trails and nearly 8 miles of off-highway motorcycle trails at the property. There are four different picnic sites on the property. All picnic sites have picnic tables available. There is a playground and volleyball nets near the swimming beach. There are six shelters and an amphitheater at Richard Bong State Recreation Area that can be reserved. All shelters can be reserved from May through October. Cross-country skiing, sledding, and ice fishing are favorite winter sports. Trails are not groomed for cross-country skiing. Richard Bong State Recreation Area is designated a Managed Hunt property.

STAMP

ROCHE-A-CRI STATE PARK

COUNTY: ADAMS   **ESTABLISHED:** 1948   **AREA (AC/HA):** 604 / 244

DATE VISITED: **LODGING:**   **WHO I WENT WITH:**

WEATHER: ☼□ ☁□ ☂□ ❄□ ⛅□ 🌬□   SPRING □ SUMMER □ FALL □ WINTER □

FEE(S):   **RATING:** ☆ ☆ ☆ ☆ ☆   **WILL I RETURN?** YES / NO

The name "Roche-A-Cri" comes from French words meaning "screaming rock." The park is centered around a 300-foot rock protrusion that features Indian petroglyphs and pictographs. The park is home to the state's only Native American rock art site. There is an access ramp that takes you to the interpretive exhibit, where you can see Native American petroglyphs and pictographs depicting ancient bird symbols. There's also a painting that shows a man and a thunderbird, one of the local gods. The park has more than 6 miles of hiking trails. The stairway to the top of the 300-foot Roche-A-Cri mound is one of the highlights of the park and offers spectacular views. Roche-A-Cri State Park has a rustic family campground open from late spring to early fall. There are three picnic areas in the park: near the office, at the steps to the mound, and at the path to Chickadee Rock. A picnic shelter with reservations is located near the steps to the mound. The main picnic shelter has a paved picnic area with an accessible grill that is located near the office parking lot and is handicap accessible. The picnic area at the park office, campground, and kiosk has playground equipment. Volleyball and horseshoe pitches are located near the picnic shelter. Anglers can head to Carter Creek, where they can find brookies and brook trout. Winter visitors can go snowshoeing and cross-country skiing on the park's trails. The main entrance is closed during the winter, and visitors should park in the parking lot on the north side of Czech Avenue, west of State Highway 13. Hunting and trapping is allowed in open areas of the park while Wisconsin State Parks hunting and trapping regulations are in effect.

STAMP

ROCK ISLAND STATE PARK

COUNTY: DOOR   **ESTABLISHED:** 1965   **AREA (AC/HA):** 912 / 369

DATE VISITED: **LODGING:**   **WHO I WENT WITH:**

WEATHER: ☀☐ ☁☐ ⛅☐ ⛈☐ 🌧☐ 🌊☐   SPRING ☐ SUMMER ☐ FALL ☐ WINTER ☐

FEE(S):   **RATING:** ☆ ☆ ☆ ☆ ☆   **WILL I RETURN?** YES / NO

The park is located on Rock Island in Lake Michigan, at the tip of the Door Peninsula. The only public transportation to the island is the Karfi passenger ferry from Washington Island. However, mooring and docking facilities are available for those with their own boats, and the island is accessible by snowmobile and foot in winter. Caution is advised as Lake Michigan can be dangerous due to reefs and storms. Dock space is limited and cannot be reserved. Kayaks and canoes are popular around the island, but lake conditions can change quickly, causing dangerous wind and waves. Early in the season (May and June), the cold water poses a particular risk of hypothermia. Canoes and kayaks can be pulled ashore near the campgrounds. All campers must register at the visitor point of contact to gain access to the campgrounds. Rock Island State Park offers primitive walk-in campsites. All supplies must be carried into and out of campsites. No vehicles are allowed on Rock Island. A fishing license is required for fishing at Rock Island State Park. Smallmouth bass and gobies are the most often caught fish. Bass season opens July 1 in the waters surrounding the islands. There are about 10 miles of trails and 6 miles of shoreline to hike on. All trails on Rock Island are open to hikers. Several shorter trails connect the campgrounds to the recreation area near the ferry landing and boathouse. Near the boathouse, there is a large playfield/picnic area with tables and grills. Rock Island has one of the most beautiful sand beaches in Door County. The water is tested regularly for safety. Swimming is permitted anywhere along the coast except near the boat dock. Many people swim from the cobble shores near their campsites. Attractions include the stone Viking boathouse and other structures including a historic water tower built by inventor Chester H. Thordarson in what is now known as the Thordarson Estate Historic District, Native American artifacts, as well as Pottawatomie Light, which is Wisconsin's oldest lighthouse. Hunting and trapping is allowed in open areas of the park while Wisconsin State Parks hunting and trapping regulations are in effect.

STAMP

ROCKY ARBOR STATE PARK

COUNTY: JUNEAU   **ESTABLISHED:** 1932   **AREA (AC/HA):** 244 / 91

DATE VISITED: **LODGING:**   **WHO I WENT WITH:**

WEATHER: ☼☐ ☁☐ ☔☐ ❄☐ ☂☐ ☁☐   SPRING ☐ SUMMER ☐ FALL ☐ WINTER ☐

FEE(S):   **RATING:** ☆ ☆ ☆ ☆ ☆   **WILL I RETURN?** YES / NO

Founded to protect the 500-million-year-old sandstone rocks that form a nearby gorge, the state park is surrounded by ancient rock formations, rich forests, and a slow-moving stream. Outdoor enthusiasts will love the 1-mile nature trail that runs through the park. You may see deer, raccoons, squirrels, bats, and chipmunks. There are wooded campsites in the park. Rocky Arbor offers a family campground that is open from Memorial Day Weekend to Labor Day Weekend. The campground has 89 wooded campsites, showers, and flush toilets. Several campsites also have electricity. The park has a picnic area and playground by the park entrance, down the hill from the campground. The park is open year round for winter hiking and snowshoeing. Hunting and trapping are allowed in the open areas of the park while Wisconsin State Parks hunting and trapping regulations are in effect.

STAMP

SAUK PRAIRIE STATE RECREATION AREA

COUNTY: SAUK   **ESTABLISHED:** 2004   **AREA (AC/HA):** 3,391 / 1,372

DATE VISITED: **LODGING:**   **WHO I WENT WITH:**

WEATHER: ☀☐ ⛅☐ 🌧☐ ❄☐ 🌩☐ 🌬☐   SPRING ☐ SUMMER ☐ FALL ☐ WINTER ☐

FEE(S):   **RATING:** ☆ ☆ ☆ ☆ ☆   **WILL I RETURN?** YES / NO

Sauk Prairie State Recreation Area was once designated as a military munitions factory that operated during World War II, the Korean War, and the Vietnam War. It was the largest munitions factory in the world during World War II. The plant was deemed beyond the needs of the military and has since been turned over to the state and other owners for recreation, conservation and research. The area offers many activities such as biking trails, off-road hiking, bird watching, and cross-country skiing. Visitors may hunt, trap, hike, pick mushrooms and berries, study nature, take photographs, and other traditional outdoor activities. You may also ride horses on the roads within the complex that are open. Please be aware of closed areas and potential hazards from construction debris and demolished structures. The recreation area is open year-round from one hour before sunrise to one hour after sunset. Roads are not cleared of snow during the winter months.

STAMP

STRAIGHT LAKE STATE PARK

COUNTY: POLK   **ESTABLISHED:** 2002   **AREA (AC/HA):** 2,000 / 809

DATE VISITED: **LODGING:**   **WHO I WENT WITH:**

WEATHER: ☀☐ ⛅☐ 🌧☐ ❄☐ 🌬☐ 🌫☐   SPRING ☐ SUMMER ☐ FALL ☐ WINTER ☐

FEE(S):   **RATING:** ☆ ☆ ☆ ☆ ☆   **WILL I RETURN?** YES / NO

Trails in this park offer views of lakes and glaciers. On the south side of the park's two wilderness lakes are ten campgrounds, boat launch sites, and a picnic area with reservations available. Campers need to practice carry-in/carry-out and should bring their own water. The park is open to the public for foot traffic only. No motorized vehicles, bikes, or horses are allowed. The Ice Age National Scenic Trail winds through the middle of the park along the Straight River and Straight Lake. There are about 8.5 miles of trail at the park. Clam Falls Trail, an abandoned road that served as an important artery during the logging era, also crosses the park roughly parallel to the Ice Age Trail. This area is excellent for bird watching. Straight Lake State Park offers a variety of recreational opportunities. In addition, the park is adjacent to a state wilderness area, resulting in nearly 3,500 acres of contiguous land at the park. Straight Lake is fed and drained by the Straight River. It is the best northern wild lake with excellent fishing for perch, northern pike, and panfish. You can fish here from a boat. Rainbow Lake is stocked with rainbow trout each year. Trout fishing is available from the first Saturday in May through the first Sunday in March. The fishing dock is located on Rainbow Lake, next to the boat landing. A fishing license is required for individuals who are 16 years of age or older. Trails are not groomed or paved during the winter. Winter hiking, snowshoeing and cross-country skiing are permitted throughout the park. Hunting and trapping is allowed in open areas of the park while Wisconsin State Parks hunting and trapping regulations are in effect.

```
STAMP
```

TOWER HILL STATE PARK

COUNTY: IOWA   ESTABLISHED: 1922   AREA (AC/HA): 77 / 31

DATE VISITED: LODGING: WHO I WENT WITH:

WEATHER: ☀☐ ⛅☐ 🌧☐ ❄☐ 🌩☐ 🌊☐   SPRING ☐ SUMMER ☐ FALL ☐ WINTER ☐

FEE(S):   RATING: ☆ ☆ ☆ ☆ ☆   WILL I RETURN? YES / NO

The park contains the reconstructed Helena Shot Tower. The original shot tower was completed in 1832 and manufactured lead shot until 1860. Visitors can see how lead shot was made in the mid-1800s and hike bluff trails. A picnic area, a large playfield, reservable shelter and a canoe landing on the Wisconsin River, and a campground are all available. There are 10 campgrounds available at Tower Hill; as of 2019, all campgrounds can be reserved. The campground is open seasonally. The park abuts the Wisconsin River and is bordered by state-owned land comprising the Lower Wisconsin State Riverway. Tower Hill State Park does not have a boat landing. The park is a popular place to explore by kayak or canoe. Fishing is available in the floodplains of the Wisconsin River. There are 2-mile trails through the park. Tower Hill is an excellent area for birdwatching enthusiasts, offering a variety of habitats with riverbanks, deep woods, and clearings. Nearby attractions include Taliesin, the American Players Theatre, the House on the Rock, and Governor Dodge State Park. Hunting and trapping is allowed in open areas of the park while Wisconsin State Parks hunting and trapping regulations are in effect.

STAMP

TURTLE-FLAMBEAU SCENIC WATERS AREA

COUNTY: IRON   **ESTABLISHED:** 1926   **AREA (AC/HA):** 40,000 / 16,187

DATE VISITED: **LODGING:**   **WHO I WENT WITH:**

WEATHER: ☀️☐ ☁️☐ 🌧️☐ ❄️☐ ⛈️☐ 🌫️☐   SPRING ☐ SUMMER ☐ FALL ☐ WINTER ☐

FEE(S):   **RATING:** ☆ ☆ ☆ ☆ ☆   **WILL I RETURN?** YES / NO

Undisturbed, wooded shorelines and islands offer the opportunity to boat, camp, fish, and enjoy the outdoors in wild and rugged northern Wisconsin. Turtle-Flambeau Scenic Waters Area offers 66 secluded camping sites accessible only by water. The family campsites and two group sites require no registration, fee, or camping permit. Six group sites are available by reservation only and require a fee. These sites are available year-round on a first-come, first-served basis. There is no fee for camping, but camping in the area is restricted to designated sites. In the past, there were many lakeside resorts located here. Today, however, most of the shoreline remains poorly developed. The Turtle-Flambeau Scenic Waters Area has six boat and kayak launch sites on the Turtle-Flambeau Flowage River. There is also a boat launch in Lake of the Falls County Park at the north end of the watercourse. The flowage provides the best of north woods fishing experiences. The flowage supports a diversity of native warm-water fish species including walleye, muskellunge, northern pike, smallmouth and largemouth bass, lake sturgeon, and various panfish species. There are five hiking trails in the Turtle-Flambeau Scenic Waters Area; there are also many miles of old logging roads to hike through the area. The Hidden Rivers Nature Trail is a 2-mile interpretive trail located off Fisherman's Landing Road. Big Island Trail, Wilson Hills Trail, and Deadhorse Trail are hiking trails for hunters, perfect for hiking any time of year. Little Turtle Trail is also a hunting trail favored by bird watchers - this trail is closed to hikers between December 15 and April 15 if the ground is covered with snow, as it is part of the MECCA cross-country trail system. The diverse topography, vegetation, and water resources of the Turtle-Flambeau Scenic Waters Area offer many hunting and trapping opportunities. The area is home to deer, bear, grouse, woodcock, turkey, grey hare, raccoon, coyote, rat, fox, mink, beaver, otter, muskrat, and a variety of waterfowl.

STAMP

WHITEFISH DUNES STATE PARK

COUNTY: DOOR **ESTABLISHED:** 1967 **AREA (AC/HA):** 867 / 349

DATE VISITED: **LODGING:** **WHO I WENT WITH:**

WEATHER: ☀☐ ☁☐ ☁☐ ☀☐ ⛈☐ ☁☐ SPRING ☐ SUMMER ☐ FALL ☐ WINTER ☐

FEE(S): **RATING:** ☆ ☆ ☆ ☆ ☆ **WILL I RETURN?** YES / NO

The park protects the fragile dune environment of Door County's eastern peninsula. At this day-use park, you can walk along Lake Michigan or along one of the many trails through the huge dunes and forest. The nature center offers year-round programs, exhibits, and demonstrations. Recreational activities include hiking, fishing, kayaking, boating, and swimming. Skiing and snowshoeing are available in the winter. When there is snow, the red, green, and yellow trails are groomed and can be skied diagonally. The black trail is open for snowshoeing. Bicycling is only allowed on designated bike paths; near the office, along the Red Trail to S. Cave Point Drive, at the Third Beach entrance to Clark Lake Road, and from the office to Schauer Road. Bicycling is not allowed on the beach/dunes or on the hiking trails. Whitefish Dunes State Park has 14.5 miles of hiking trails. Do not enter the dunes and stay on designated trails and steps to protect the rare plant and animal species that are home to Whitefish Dunes. The park features 1.5 miles of sandy beach. The beach shores are a great place to walk, view the dunes and enjoy the waters of Lake Michigan. Swimming is available in Lake Michigan. No lifeguards are present. There is no boat launch in the park. Users of small watercraft or floatation devices should be aware of wind conditions on Lake Michigan. Fishing is available in Clark Lake. The Clark Lake Spur trail provides access to Clark Lake from within the park. Fishing licenses are required. Anglers of all ages may rent basic fishing equipment at no charge from the park office. The picnic area at Whitefish Dunes State Park features charcoal grills, picnic tables, a shelter building with reservations, and a drinking fountain. This area is located near the parking lot overlooking the Lake Michigan shoreline. Hunting and trapping is allowed in open areas of the park while Wisconsin State Parks hunting and trapping regulations are in effect.

STAMP

WILDCAT MOUNTAIN STATE PARK

COUNTY: VERNON **ESTABLISHED:** 1948 **AREA (AC/HA):** 3,643 / 1,474

DATE VISITED: **LODGING:** **WHO I WENT WITH:**

WEATHER: ☼□ ☁□ 🌧□ ❄□ ⛅□ 🌬□ SPRING □ SUMMER □ FALL □ WINTER □

FEE(S): **RATING:** ☆ ☆ ☆ ☆ ☆ **WILL I RETURN?** YES / NO

The park sits on the edge of a hill overlooking the majestic Kickapoo River Valley. The Kickapoo River, which is over 100 miles long, is the longest tributary of the Wisconsin River. The park offers dense forests, a crystal clear river, and streams, boasts a spectacular landscape, offering visitors the opportunity to fish, hike, and picnic in the area. Wildcat Mountain State Park offers camping for families, groups, and horseback riders. Twenty-one miles of scenic hiking, nature, and equestrian trails run through the park. The park has two compass orienteering trails developed by the Eagle Scout. The long trail is 1.33 miles long and the short trail is 1.05 miles long. Compasses can be rented at the park office. Wildcat Mountain State Park has several horse trail loops totaling 15 miles and offers 24 horse camping sites available northeast of the park office on Taylor Valley Road. There are no horses for rent at the park. A lookout point and picnic areas offer views of the Kickapoo Valley. The Kickapoo River is a popular place to paddle, and equipment rentals can be found in the Village of Ontario. The Kickapoo River is known for its miles of slow-moving water that flows through wild areas. The river attracts kayaking enthusiasts to the park. Kayakers can observe the rare plants that grow on the banks of the river and watch the wildlife that live on the banks, including muskrats, banded kingfishers, green herons, and blue herons. The Kickapoo River between Ontario and Gays Mills has a total of 46 fish species, including an abundance of brown trout. Anglers of any age may check out basic fishing equipment free of charge at the park office. Wildcat Mountain State Park has an upper picnic area with a reservable shelter and playground, a lower picnic area along the Kickapoo River with a shelter (non-reservable), and a picnic area at the Ice Cave trail parking lot. There are two shelters and an amphitheater at Wildcat Mountain State Park. Wildcat Mountain State Park offers beauty and recreational opportunities for visitors throughout the year. There are 7 miles of cross-country ski trails in the park. Skiers can begin and end their runs at the park office or maintenance building. The 2.5-mile Old-Settlers hiking trail loop is converted to a snowshoe trail in winter. Hunting and trapping is allowed in open areas of the park while Wisconsin State Parks hunting and trapping regulations are in effect.

STAMP

WILLOW RIVER STATE PARK

COUNTY: ST. CROIX   **ESTABLISHED:** 1967   **AREA (AC/HA):** 2,800 / 1,133

DATE VISITED: **LODGING:**   **WHO I WENT WITH:**

WEATHER: ☀☐ ⛅☐ ☁☐ ❄☐ ☂☐ 〰☐   SPRING ☐ SUMMER ☐ FALL ☐ WINTER ☐

FEE(S):   **RATING:** ☆ ☆ ☆ ☆ ☆   **WILL I RETURN?** YES / NO

The waterfall is the park's most popular attraction. Willow Falls cascades 200 feet down into a deep gorge. Another popular feature is Little Falls Lake, a shallow reservoir on the Willow River. Trilobite fossils found in the lower layers of the gorge indicate the rock is around 600 million years old. The park includes the following recreational activities: camping, fishing, boating, swimming, rock climbing, biking, and hiking. There are 11 trails in the park with over 13 miles of trails. The trails vary in difficulty. The park has 2 miles of paved trails on the north side of the river, available for pet owners and activities such as snowshoeing, dog sledding, and hiking. The most popular hiking destination is Willow Falls and the scenic views of the river valley. At Willow River State Park, the Hidden Ponds Nature Trail is wheelchair accessible. The park also offers wheelchair accessible campsites and a fishing pier. Some warm water species such as panfish, bass, and northern can be found below the dam. The Willow River is stocked with trout. Trout fishing is likely best upstream of the waterfall. Bicycling is permitted on the paved Little Falls Trail, designated single-track mountain bike trails, and park roads. There is a swimming beach on Little Falls Lake. The Willow River is accessible in many places, but there are no other designated swimming areas within the park. Boating, kayaking, and canoeing are popular on Little Falls Lake. There is a boat landing on the lake. Rentals are available in season. It is possible to kayak on the river, but kayakers should be careful of changing river conditions and underwater debris. Other surrounding lakes and the St. Croix River offer motorized boating opportunities. Willow River's campground, on the southern shore of Little Falls Lake, is very popular and has one of the highest occupancy rates in the Wisconsin State Park System. Willow River State Park has picnic areas with tables and grills at several locations throughout the park. The largest picnic area is at the beach at Little Falls Lake. No pets are allowed in the picnic area on the beach, but there is a pet area with tables and grills at the boat launch. There are three playgrounds at Willow River State Park: the beach picnic area, Campground 100, and Campground 300. The beach picnic area also has large areas of open grass for sports and recreation. At Willow River State Park, there is a shelter near the picnic area at the dam with reservations available. There is also a shelter at the beach area that can be used on a first-come, first-served basis. Hunting and trapping are allowed in the open areas of the park while Wisconsin State Parks hunting and trapping regulations are in effect.

STAMP

WYALUSING STATE PARK

COUNTY: GRANT   **ESTABLISHED:** 1917   **AREA (AC/HA):** 2,628 / 1,064

DATE VISITED: **LODGING:**   **WHO I WENT WITH:**

WEATHER: ☀☐ ☁☐ ☔☐ ❄☐ 🌬☐ 〰☐   SPRING ☐ SUMMER ☐ FALL ☐ WINTER ☐

FEE(S):   **RATING:** ☆ ☆ ☆ ☆ ☆   **WILL I RETURN?** YES / NO

Wyalusing means "home of the warrior" in the Lenape language spoken by Munsee-Delaware tribes who settled in the area in the 19th century after being displaced from farther east. Famous for its steep, panoramic bluffs, Wyalusing State Park is located at the junction of the Mississippi and Wisconsin Rivers. Rising more than 500 feet above the river valley, the bluffs are a birdwatcher's paradise, home to more than 90 species of birds. The two mountain bike trails in Wyalusing (Whitetail Meadows and Mississippi Ridge) are not designed for high speeds. They can become soft and slippery when wet and can erode quickly during heavy rains. The park has a boat landing from which boats can be launched. Motorized boats are permitted. Boats can be rented from companies near Bagley and in the Prairie du Chien area. There is no beach at the state park, but there is a beach, boat landing, and picnic area at Wyalusing Recreation Area, 2 miles south of the park entrance. There is a municipal swimming area in Prairie du Chien. A canoe trail through the river floodplains is a unique way to observe waterfowl, aquatic plants and a variety of bottom-dwelling animals. The trail begins and ends at the park's boat landing. The Mississippi and Wisconsin river backwaters offer excellent fishing for panfish, bass, northern pike, and walleye. There's an accessible fishing pier at the boat landing. Wyalusing offers several camping options for visitors, including two family campsites, an outdoor group camp, and the Hugh Harper indoor group camp. Wyalusing has over 14 miles of hiking trails. The trails can vary in difficulty. Wyalusing State Park has several picnic areas and shelters. The central picnic area is near the entrance to the Wisconsin Ridge campground. There are several tables at the Peterson shelter and at the playground across from the shelter. Other picnic areas include the Homestead picnic area, the Henneger Point picnic area, and the Green Cloud picnic area. There is a playground at the entrance to the Wisconsin Ridge campground. Wyalusing State Park has five open shelters that can be reserved for group activities. Wyalusing State Park offers many cross-country ski trails for all levels of skiers. All trails are accessible from the Astronomy Center parking lot. Ski trails include Turkey Hollow, Whitetail Meadows and Prairie. Cross-country skiers can enjoy beautiful views of the mighty Mississippi River from Cathedral Tree Drive. Hunting and trapping is allowed in open areas of the park while Wisconsin State Parks hunting and trapping regulations are in effect.

STAMP

YELLOWSTONE LAKE STATE PARK

COUNTY: LAFAYETTE   **ESTABLISHED:** 1970   **AREA (AC/HA):** 968 / 392

DATE VISITED: **LODGING:**   **WHO I WENT WITH:**

WEATHER: ☀☐ ⛅☐ 🌧☐ ❄☐ ⛈☐ 🌥☐   SPRING ☐ SUMMER ☐ FALL ☐ WINTER ☐

FEE(S):   **RATING:** ☆ ☆ ☆ ☆ ☆   **WILL I RETURN?** YES / NO

The park is a popular year-round recreational area that offers visitors plenty of space for camping, swimming, fishing, boating, hiking, biking, and picnicking. In the winter, the park is open for ice fishing, snowmobiling, and cross-country skiing. The adjacent Yellowstone Wildlife Area also offers additional recreational activities, including horse trails and a shooting range. Yellowstone Lake State Park offers 4 miles of off-road bicycle trails. The roads and trails in the park are heavily used, so bicyclists should always watch out for traffic and pedestrians. The 455-acre lake is accessible to boats, canoes, kayaks, sailboats, and other watercraft. There are two boat launch ramps and one kayak launch. At the east end of the lake, there is a food court and a boat rental facility that can be used in the summer. Yellowstone Lake has a designated swimming beach and a bathhouse nearby. No lifeguards are on duty. Yellowstone Lake has both family and group campsites. Yellowstone Lake has an abundant population of crappies, walleye, and other gamefish. Fishing opportunities also exist for bass, bluegill, channel catfish, muskies, and northern pike. Yellowstone Lake has more than 13 miles of hiking trails. Trails may vary in difficulty. Steep climbs or descents and stairways may be encountered. The main trailhead is located at the bottom of Campground Hill Road. There are nine designated picnic areas. A picnic shelter is located at the west end of the lake and can be rented. There are no trash or recycling garbage cans in the day use or picnic areas, so please remember the carry in, carry out rule. Pets are not allowed in the picnic areas, beach areas, or playgrounds. There are designated pet areas west of the beach. You may reserve a shelter on the west side of the picnic area at Yellowstone Lake. The shelter is accessible and has electricity. There are 5 miles of trails in the park that are groomed and maintained for cross-country skiing when conditions and personnel permit. A Wisconsin State Park trail pass is not required at Yellowstone Lake, but a vehicle sticker is required. Hunting and trapping are allowed in the open areas of the park while Wisconsin State Parks hunting and trapping regulations are in effect.

STAMP

PHOTOS   PARK NAME...

PHOTOS   PARK NAME..

PHOTOS   PARK NAME..

PHOTOS   PARK NAME...

PHOTOS   PARK NAME..

PHOTOS   PARK NAME...

PHOTOS   PARK NAME...

PHOTOS   PARK NAME...

PHOTOS   PARK NAME...

PHOTOS   PARK NAME..

Thank you for taking the time to read my book. I hope you found it enjoyable.

Your feedback is important to me, and I would greatly appreciate it if you could take a moment to share your thoughts by leaving an online review.

Your review will not only help me improve as an author but also assist other potential readers in making informed decisions.

Once again, thank you for your support and for considering leaving a review.

Warm regards,

Max Kukis Galgan

Write to me if you think I should improve anything in my book:

maxkukisgalgan@gmail.com

SEE OTHER BOOKS

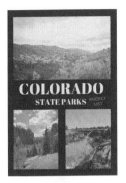

MISSOURI
STATE PARKS BUCKET LIST

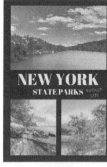

NEW YORK
STATE PARKS BUCKET LIST

OHIO
STATE PARKS BUCKET LIST

OREGON
STATE PARKS BUCKET LIST

PENNSYLVANIA
STATE PARKS BUCKET JOURNAL

TENNESSEE
STATE PARKS BUCKET LIST

TEXAS
STATE PARKS BUCKET LIST

UTAH
STATE PARKS BUCKET LIST

VIRGINIA
STATE PARKS BUCKET LIST

WASHINGTON
STATE PARKS BUCKET LIST

WISCONSIN
STATE PARKS BUCKET LIST

Made in the USA
Monee, IL
21 June 2024